THE
GOOD HOUSE

Man's position in a world of contrasts is represented in this painted Blackfoot Indian tepee. The black area at the bottom is the earth, and the larger black area at the top is the heavens (with dots of white stars and a striped rainbow). The structural poles themselves link the earth and heavens, acting as the paths for man's prayers, ascending to the spirits.

THE GOOD HOUSE

Contrast as a design tool

Max Jacobson ▪ Murray Silverstein ▪ Barbara Winslow

The Taunton Press

Cover illustration: Murray Silverstein

Photos and drawings by the authors, except where noted

...by fellow enthusiasts

First printing: October 1990
Printed in the United States of America

A FINE HOMEBUILDING Book

Fine Homebuilding® is a trademark of The Taunton Press, Inc.
registered in the U.S. Patent and Trademark Office.

The Taunton Press, 63 South Main Street, Box 5506,
Newtown, CT 06740-5506

Library of Congress Cataloging-in-Publication Data

Jacobson, Max, 1941-
    The good house : contrast as a design tool / Max Jacobson, Murray
Silverstein and Barbara Winslow.
        p.   cm.
    "A Fine homebuilding book" — T.p. verso.
    ISBN 0-942391-05-5 : $21.95
    1. Architecture, Domestic. 2. Architectural design.
    I. Silverstein, Murray. II. Winslow, Barbara, 1941-
    III. Title.
NA7115.J33   1990   90-11056
728 — dc20   CIP

CONTENTS

FOREWORD

Interest in the individually designed house, especially the house designed to be a part of everyday life, seems in danger of being obliterated by either an interest in the house as an ingredient in a general trend toward consumerism, or as narrow polemic — the house designed, consciously or not, to be apart from life.

The tradition of the house as a central part of architectural practice is long and important — and for good reasons, reasons beyond the obvious essential ones of satisfying particular needs in particular settings. The best reason for the designer may be the way in which the design of a particular house leads to more important realities beyond purely formal intentions, simply because one is working with real people on a real site. When one designs a house, the user is not imagined or removed, but rather real and there, a participant at one's shoulder. In the absence of an identifiable user (much architectural design, especially public or development work, is for an unknown or unknowable user), designers tend to convert real-life problems into surrogate formal problems. In the individually designed house, the presence of the user gives the whole process an inescapable immediacy, and the good designer does what always should be done — use architecture to solve problems larger and more real than academic ones.

Books on the design and building of houses abound, and there is a long tradition of such writing; Vitruvius can be read as being about the design of houses. Recently, books on houses have tended to be either collections of images — written, drawn or photographic — often with little explanation as to how the houses got that way; or they are building manuals, again paying little attention to design. Others have been polemic works that use the house as a means toward a particular theoretical end, in which both the house and its occupants are irrelevant.

In *The Good House*, the focus is on the house as something to be lived in and enjoyed. This thoughtful book by a group of serious practitioners reflecting on their own varied experiences, is an important contribution. While the book moves from theory to practice, the authors worked the other way around: practicing first, then developing theory. Indeed the book could be read backwards, the last chapters on practice first, then the first chapters on theory. The task the authors have set

themselves — to describe what goes into designing a good house — is not easy; describing the design process never is. The authors' notion of contrast is important, as either a dialectic of two contrasting elements of the design or a dialectic produced by contrasting a single designed element with existing natural elements — views, the qualities of light, the site itself — so that both built and natural elements are more acutely enjoyed and understood. It is indeed only by contrast that the world is readable at all.

— *Joseph Esherick, FAIA*
San Francisco
July 1990

PREFACE

We are architects who have spent much of the last 16 years designing and building houses. We have worked for families, developers, institutions, government agencies, and for ourselves; we have built from the ground up and made additions and alterations to existing homes. On occasion we have worked with generous budgets, but more often on shoestrings. Perhaps the central question we have sought to answer in our work is, quite simply, "What constitutes good house design?" That is, what is it about the physical form of a dwelling that makes it a good place to be in — supportive, vibrant and appealing to both the intellect and the senses?

When we undertook the writing of this book, our aim was to explore this question in a practical way, by analyzing where certain projects succeed in being strong and memorable, and where they fail. Through this exercise, we hoped to extrapolate a series of design strategies that readers could manipulate to enrich the character of many different kinds of dwelling. Setting to work, we soon realized that many of the concepts we wished to discuss were related. Indeed, we began to see that the design strategies we find most important — both in our work and in the work of others — could all be seen as variations on a single underlying theme: the theme of contrast. Strong design seems to grow from elements in a state of contrast at all scales. From the overall shape of a building down to the details of trim, a good house is composed of sharply contrasting qualities, all working together. For example, to create a room that is light and expansive, also create (to some degree) its opposite, a place that is dark and enclosed. And then link the two. Likewise, to experience warmth we need the cold; to experience order we need mystery. Good design, in these terms, is the production of harmony through the orchestration of strong contrasts.

This book reflects our commitment to generating a series of useful design strategies. To this end, we show how and to what purpose a wide range of ideas has been applied in built projects — our own and those of other people. But we also think of this book as an excursion into architectural theory, and hope readers will join us in examining the notion that all the concepts we discuss converge and contain an underlying coherence (in the theory of contrast). This theoretical examination also has a practical benefit, for it is our experience that the struggle to find coherence of any sort in design produces new insights. Looking at dwellings in the context of a theory

of contrast has deepened our understanding of them and strengthened our own designs.

The book is organized into two sections, "Theory" and "Practice." The first section introduces the theory of contrast and its relationship to residential design, then goes on to explicate a collection of design strategies. The second section contains analyses of four very different residences by other architects, as well as samples of our own work, which demonstrate step by step how theory and strategy figure in both design and the final building.

We have written this book for anyone interested in residential architecture, design and construction. We have imagined our readership to consist of architects, students, designers, owner-builders, contractors and developers. No theoretical or technical preparation is required, and we have tried to avoid specialized or technical language. We spend part of our time teaching architectural design as well as practicing it, and have developed some of the material from our work with students; we hope other educators will find it useful in their studio work.

ACKNOWLEDGMENTS

Many people have helped us with this book. Charles Miller, our friend and West Coast editor of *Fine Homebuilding* magazine, originally proposed the project and brought us together with The Taunton Press. He first spent time with us discussing what the book should cover, then read the first drafts. Throughout, he offered encouragement and insight; we are greatly indebted to him.

Several individuals helped by allowing us to visit and photograph their homes, and by discussing their experiences and understanding of these buildings. Thanks go to Westin Havens (who commissioned his house from Harwell Hamilton Harris in 1939), to Sandy Hodges and Lisa Staedlhofer (the current owners of Maybeck's Schneider house) and to Drs. Larry and Michelle Corash, the current owners of the Penn house.

We thank those individuals and groups that granted permission to reprint various materials. We especially appreciate the cooperation of those architects and artists who so generously donated material from their offices and personal collections: included are Gary Coates and Susanne Siepl-Coates, Abdel Wahed El-Wakil, Harwell Hamilton Harris, Suzanne

Crowhurst Lennard, Richard Peters, Jesse Reichek, William Turnbull and Forrest Wilson.

Three university curators and their collections deserve special thanks: Kate Ware at the Oakland Museum for her help in obtaining photos from the Roger Sturtevant Collection; Caitlin King for her help with the Documents Collection at the College of Environmental Design, University of California, Berkeley; and Lila Stillson at the University of Texas at Austin for her help with the Harris Collection.

This book was written in our office, at the same time that we were carrying on our architectural practice. The people who work with us have been extremely understanding, helping us with the inevitably conflicting demands of such an enterprise. They have provided us with intellectual support and a collegial atmosphere: thanks to Laurie Erickson, Ken Martin, Martha Jain, Doug Shaffer, Alfredo Botello and Helen Degenhardt. Particular thanks to those who worked directly on the manuscript and illustrations: Ricardo Cavernelis, who spent a couple of months obtaining prints and photo rights, and Katharine Fisher and Melissa Harris, who did several of the diagrams and drawings for the book.

A special thanks to all of our clients over the years who have helped us to forge the ideas presented in this book, and particularly to those whose homes and projects are included here as examples.

Finally, it has been a pleasure working with the people at The Taunton Press. They have been a source of practical help, vision and good will over the last few years. Paul Bertorelli helped to clarify and focus the project whenever it seemed lost in the doldrums, and freelance editor Laura Tringali helped pull it all together, providing invaluable editorial assistance during the last phase of writing.

SECTION 1:
THEORY

1

GOOD HOUSES AND THE THEORY OF CONTRAST

Most of the houses we see every day are certainly adequate. They're built with competence according to the building code, they keep out the weather, they're perfectly nice—but no more. Other houses, far fewer in number, have a more powerful impact. They go beyond competence and are satisfying in deeper ways—aesthetically, emotionally, intellectually, perhaps even spiritually. Such houses not only offer protection from the extremes of winter and summer, but also facilitate the enjoyment of nature's elements. While containing the required number and size of spaces, they are also organized to improve the quality of social life together and private hours apart. These "good houses" have the capacity to awaken the senses, memories and minds of their occupants, and inspire productive energies.

A famous story is told of the Zen novitiate whose task was to sweep the monastery path clean. He couldn't understand why his teacher wasn't satisfied with his immaculate product until the teacher sprinkled a few leaves on the path. Then he understood the experience of 'clean.' This garden path contrasts flat and hilly, massive and delicate, dark and light, organic and inorganic. (Photo © 1989 Robert Stolk.)

relation to a sense of warmth, cozy containment is experienced with reference to soaring openness, and the awareness of light is anchored by darkness.

In life it is the mixture of male/female, dark/light, hard/soft, in/out and so on that creates all the excitement. In fact, these contrasts create a new experience or existence—a child, a sensation, a texture, a feeling. An examination of even simple objects demonstrates this clearly. It is the blend of warp and weft threads that make up a fabric—without opposites there are only two balls of thread. In creating a bowl, the potter begins with a lump of clay; only by creating an in/out contrast can the clay become a useful vessel. The builders of the first huts shaped an inside space with solid materials and discovered that they had simultaneously created a new exterior space, a world that could be measured in distances to and from this new center.

In addition, the links between contrasts allow a building to be responsive to the ever-changing needs of its occupants. For example, when they are active, they are warm, but when they rest, they begin to feel chilled. If a basically cool room can be linked to the warmth of the sun by a south-facing window bay, each person then has the opportunity to find a position at the precise point of real equilibrium and comfort. In this sense, the building is better able to support its inhabitants.

By the same token, linked contrasts offer the opportunity for change and growth. The child on the front porch (the link between home and the outside world) can either retreat into the house for safety or venture out into the world beyond for adventure and learning. The good house, then, by providing simultaneous security and opportunity, encourages the full experience of life. You are willing to deepen your experience by enjoying a chilly breath of outdoor air if you can anticipate the waiting warmth of the fire. Likewise, you can relish private contemplation alone in a small room, knowing that the family can be rejoined nearby. You can delight in the idiosyncratic aspects of a building if they exist in relation to a logical order.

We have said that the linkages are themselves architectural elements or parts of the building. As a corollary, the parts of a building should also be thought of as links between other contrasting elements. For example, the front yard is the link between public and private realms; the lampshade is the link between light and dark; the column's capital is the link between the lintel and the

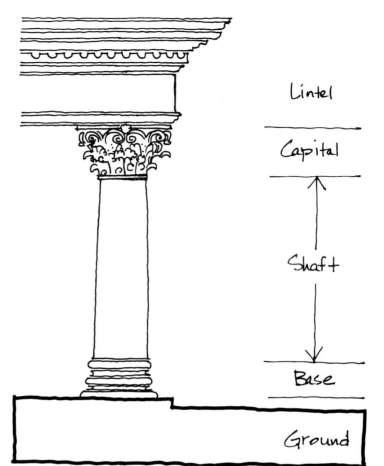

The lintel above and the ground below are linked by the supporting column. At a smaller scale of detail, the contrast between the horizontal lintel and vertical shaft is linked by the capital. Similarly, the base is the link between the vertical shaft and the horizontal ground.

shaft, while the base is the link between the shaft and the ground. Awareness of this concept of linkages will enrich and inform the design of each part of a building.

Finally, the presence of contrast at all levels of scale answers the human need for continuity of orientation, ensuring a sense of connection to the surrounding environment. As we sit in a room, it is important to be able to feel its connection to the

The broad roof overhang and stone steps link this Japanese house to its surrounding garden.

larger house and yard. Otherwise, there can be disorientation (like the momentary confusion when awakening in a strange house). Similarly, we need to be able to see a room's textural components (the texture of the walls, for example), so that we can orient ourselves in a material world. When we feel oriented and part of the world, we are encouraged to explore, to open ourselves to different ranges of experience.

Contrast and Design Development

Even with just this brief introduction, it should now be possible to set this book aside momentarily and use the theory of contrast to begin designing the elements of the world around you. For example, try to:

1. recognize where more contrast is needed between any two parts of your surroundings, and try to create that contrast;

2. create a link between the contrasted parts; and

3. extend this work to both larger and smaller scales.

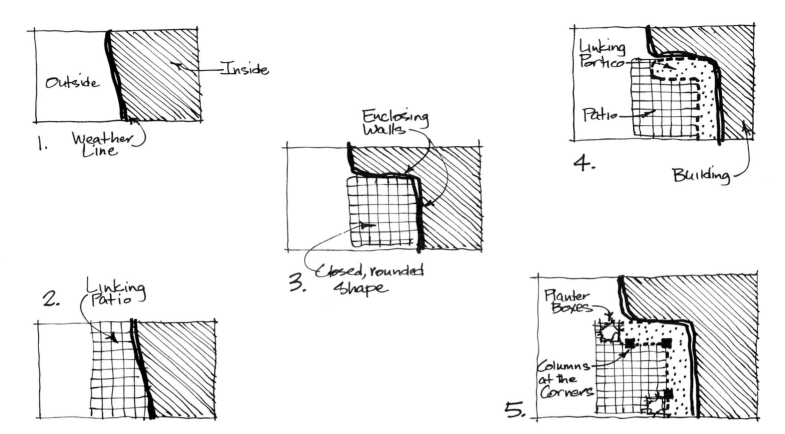

1. Outside — Inside
Weather Line

2. Linking Patio

3. Closed, rounded Shape
Enclosing Walls

4. Linking Portico
Patio
Building

5. Planter Boxes
Columns at the Corners

As you think about a site plan, for example, start by sharply contrasting the inside with the outside spaces using a complete, closed weather line. Then link inside and outside with a new element, say a patio. Create more contrast between this patio and everything else in the design by giving it a closed, rounded shape and by partially enclosing it with solid walls. Later on in the design, when you are working on the next smallest scale, return to the patio and link it more strongly to the house by creating a new linking part, say a covered portico along the patio/building edge. Later, contrast the portico with the larger patio by placing columns and planter boxes at the portico/patio edge. Continue to contrast and differentiate as you proceed to link and integrate.

This sequence of sketches shows how the theory of contrast can be used to help generate an outdoor patio.

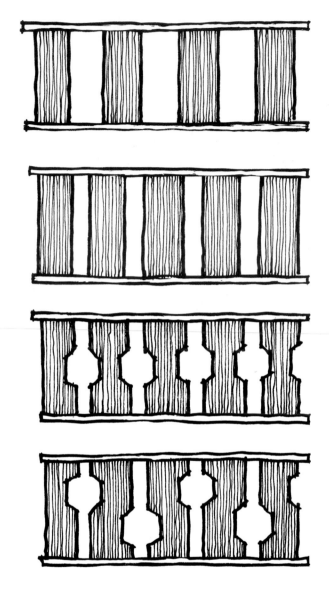

To bring contrast to the design of a deck railing:
(A) Create contrast between the boards and the spaces between them.
(B) Eliminate strict balance to enliven contrast. Here, the gaps are a little narrower than the boards.
(C) Bind the contrasts together with a new part, here, a hexagon shape in the gap.
(D) Contrast adjacent hexagons by alternately raising and lowering their positions.

A.

B.

C.

D.

For another example, assume that you are trying to come up with a deck-railing design using wide boards. By introducing the contrast between solid and void and then linking them with shape, it is possible to create an interesting pattern, as shown in the drawing above.

Looking at things with the theory of contrast foremost in mind almost automatically enhances design development. If you simply pay attention to the need for contrasting parts and then mediate and link them together, you will start to create vital new elements of a building.

The Six Dimensions of Contrast

In the next six chapters, we will present the most important dimensions of contrast in the design and experience of the good house. They include, for example, the dimensions of in/out, light/dark and order/mystery. For each one, we will try to identify design strategies that will enable you successfully to incorporate that dimension of contrast into an architectural design.

Chapter 8, which concludes the theoretical section of the book, shows that the dimensions of contrast are not independent variables, but are related and interconnected to one another. The use of any one of the dimensions in design will invite corresponding uses of other dimensions. In the good house, these contrasts are orchestrated to be in harmony with one another, to form a contrasting whole.

2
INSIDE AND OUTSIDE

Inside and outside form an inseparable pair — you cannot have one without the other. When you create an inside, you automatically shape an outside. With each stroke, the designer of a building creates inside, outside and the relationship between them; architecture's primary role is to provide the requisite contrast of in/out, and then to link the two in a balanced relationship.

We need the inside to establish physical security and identity, and safety from nature's elements and society's demands. We need the outside to interact with the world and society, and to get nurturing inputs of sun, air and food. But the feeling of being in or out is not limited to being physically indoors or outdoors. In a forest you can feel very much inside; likewise, if your viewpoint is from an empty adjacent dining room, you can feel very much outside a crowded kitchen.

What makes a place feel inside or outside? What does the host mean when, after taking your coat in the entry, he says, "Come on in"? Weren't you already in? When Frank Lloyd Wright visited Philip Johnson's glass house, he told Johnson that he didn't know whether to take off his hat or leave it on. And isn't it true that many spaces lack strength as either inside or outside places, and are neither here nor there? In cities, we long for the presence of nature, adding greenhouses and sliding-glass doors to our dewllings. In wilderness areas, the challenge is to tame the surroundings by establishing a solid interior feeling.

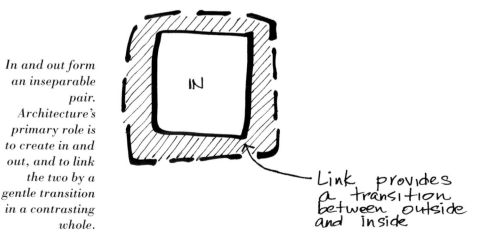

In and out form an inseparable pair. Architecture's primary role is to create in and out, and to link the two by a gentle transition in a contrasting whole.

OUT

IN

Link provides a transition between outside and inside

Here we consider the four major tools that can be used to create the feeling of inside/outside. To make a space feel more interior, you can increase its concavity, give definition to its corners and edges, increase opacity, decrease its size and make it accessible through a series of layers. Conversely, to create a space more exterior in character, you can increase its convexity and transparency, and open it up. Let's look at these strategies.

Concave and Convex Shapes

From any viewpoint within an architectural space, it is possible to look around in all directions and determine whether the space is essentially concave or convex. Here's a useful rule of thumb: The feeling of inside is increased by concavity; the feeling of outside is increased by convexity. A concave ceiling, such as a vault or simple peak, increases the feeling of in-ness, but an L-shaped living area feels more open and less cozy because of the convex angle of the wall projecting into the room. To increase the feeling of being inside, bend the walls so that they wrap around the occupants. Increase the feeling of being outside by thrusting the exterior walls outward.

Defined and Undefined Boundaries

If the corners or edges of a space are clearly defined, we will feel we are inside something. If we cannot perceive the boundaries of the space, we'll feel less enclosed.

An outdoor space can be made to feel more interior simply by defining its corners, boundaries and limits more strongly. An interior room can be made to feel more spacious and open to the exterior by rounding off its corners and edges.

Opaque and Transparent Surfaces

The feeling of inside is increased by opacity; the feeling of outside is increased by transparency. To illustrate, imagine yourself within a cube that has surfaces covered with varying proportions of brick and glass. You can see that the greater the number of opaque surfaces, the more interior the space will feel. Take the same space, add a pitched roof and imagine it rendered in two contrasting opacities—first as a stone cairn with walls 2 ft. thick, and second as a delicate pavilion formed of a few poles and a little lath. Because the stone building buffers all outside stimulation, its occupants will feel more inside than in the pavilion, which is almost completely open.

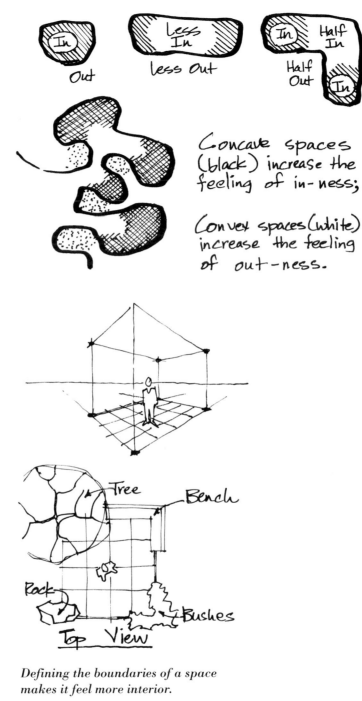

Concave spaces (black) increase the feeling of in-ness;

Convex spaces (white) increase the feeling of out-ness.

Define in and out by using varying degrees of concavity and convexity. Concave spaces (black) increase the feeling of in-ness; convex spaces (white) increase the feeling of out-ness.

Defining the boundaries of a space makes it feel more interior.

13

HERE ——————————————→ THERE

*The personal
sense of a
here/there axis
can organize
one's spatial
experience of in
and out.*

The architectural dimension of in/out can be related to a personal sense of in/out. Imagine an axis of in/out, starting with your body at the center and extending radially outward into the world. The drawing at left illustrates a scale of size in that a room is bigger than a body but smaller than a neighborhood. Because a small room is closer to our bodies, we tend to feel more inside in smaller spaces, less inside in larger spaces. This is perhaps because our sense of inside begins with our bodies, then extends to our clothes and from there proceeds outward to the surrounding spaces.

This diagram has another feature: As you go outward from room to building to yard to street, the sense of moving outside will be increased if each level is marked with a transition, barrier or gate, creating onion-like layers of in/out. Likewise, the sense of inside will be increased if the building is comprised of layers proceeding from entry to public area to living room to alcove. These layers encourage a sense of depth — how deep in or how far out.

14

Linking In and Out

Now let's consider the ways in and out can be linked to form a contrasting whole. Here are strategies we find useful in our work.

In Stands Alone in a Field of Out

This is the simplest strategy of all. The building stands fortress-like, isolated in the landscape, creating a central focal point around which nature radiates outward. As Rudolf Arnheim writes in *The Dynamics of Architectural Form* (Berkeley: University of California Press, 1977; p. 215): "…a tower on a hill creates an accent around which nature may organize itself in a comprehensible order." Obviously, this technique works only for fairly isolated buildings. In/out are linked here through radial geometry (see p. 60), by distance to the centered building. That land near to the building—with its porches, decks and tended gardens—links the inside with the wilder land beyond.

A variation of this technique on smaller sites is to design the house so it appears to be a platform floating in nature. An example is shown in the photo at right. This approach can be used even on tight city lots, where the house "floats" at the center of a front and rear yard.

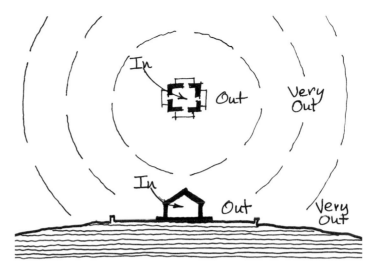

In stands alone in a field of out.

The Budge house by Charles Moore and William Turnbull (1966) is a simple pavilion—an inside that, with its panel walls raised, seems to float in a sea of outside. (Photo © Morley Baer.)

In cradles out.

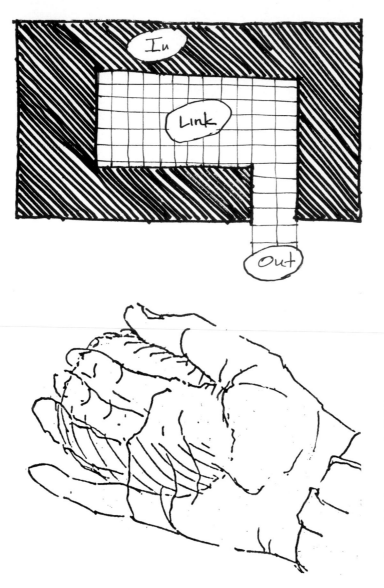

In Cradles Out

This is conceptually the opposite relationship: Out stands alone in a field of in. It is a courtyard scheme, where the building wraps around the edge of the site, capturing a piece of the outdoors. This captured space becomes the link between the building and the world beyond. In cities, courtyard schemes may be stacked one against another to form blocks; in the country, such buildings often stand alone, as in the strategy shown in the drawing at left, where, paradoxically, the outside court is experienced as the most interior place.

In and Out Interlock

The previous two strategies stress separateness and oppositeness. At the other extreme, in/out can interlock so evenly and democratically that neither one dominates. Those exterior spaces that are strongly shaped by the building become the link between the inside and the world beyond.

A characteristic of such compositions is that they tend to possess figure/ground reversal, like the black-and-white Gestalt diagrams that may be seen as both a white figure on a black ground and vice versa. Indeed, designers searching for this

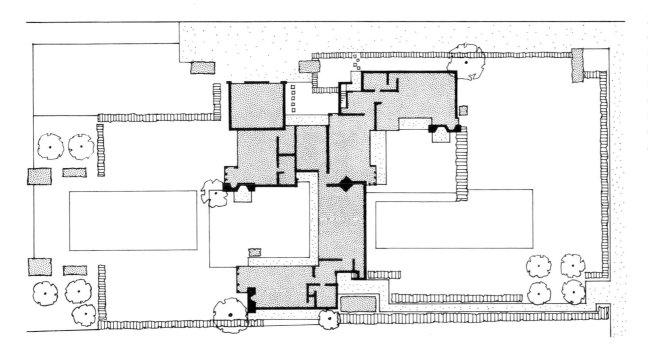

*In this site plan
of the Rudolf
Schindler house
in Los Angeles
(1922), interiors
and exteriors
interlock to form
a strong weave
of in/out.*

interlocking quality in their site plans will often squint at their early sketches to see if they flip in precisely this way. This may seem like a formal quality that only architects see on the drawing board, but it can lead to buildings that, like the Schindler house (whose plan is shown in the drawing above), are experienced as a strong weave of in/out.

Inside
Enfronts Outside

This strategy and the ones that follow are based on geometrical relationships. If a building establishes a geometrical order, then that order will radiate outward into the landscape. When we are outside, we can

be made to feel the geometry of the inside; when inside, we will sense the building's order radiating out into the landscape beyond.

The interior of a typical single-family dwelling is linked to the outer world by front and rear yards; neither yard is as outside in the public sense as the street. These yards are defined by fences, paths and plantings, but most of all, by the building facades that enfront them. Think of the yard as a room, one wall of which is the enfronting exterior facade of the building. The yard-room can then be developed as a space whose plan organization and volumetric proportions are related to the defining wall. In this way, the front and rear facades of a building

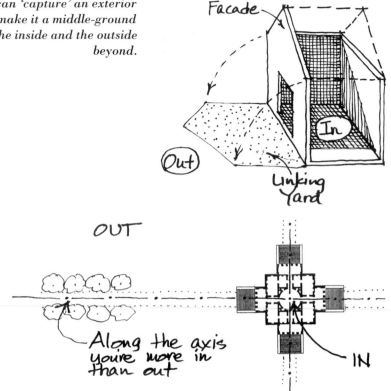

A facade can 'capture' an exterior space and make it a middle-ground link between the inside and the outside beyond.

Facade

Out

In

Linking Yard

OUT

Along the axis you're more in than out

IN

The building's strong symmetry organizes the outside around it. If you step off the axis, you are really outside. But on the axis, you are on a conceptual carpet leading to the building, and in this sense you are less outside than if you were at an unrelated point.

can be made to capture their yards, taming them, and thus forging a link between pure outside and pure inside. Such yards can be thought of as transformations of the front and rear facades of the building projected down onto the ground. The dimensions of the yard space are thus proportional to the dimensions of the facade. A tall facade will establish a deep yard, a wide facade suggests a wide yard. The tall, squarish facades of Old West storefronts created strong, deep front spaces.

Adjoining townhouses can create especially strong yards because the definitions of nearby spaces are cumulative — the spaces don't have a chance to dissipate at the gaps between buildings. In effect, there are no side yards to reduce the impact of the front yards.

Axes of Symmetry

If a building establishes an axis of symmetry, residents will sense being on-axis or off-axis as they stand outside facing the building. Similarly, when inside a symmetrically organized room, inhabitants will feel the axis extending beyond the room, out into the surrounding landscape. Thus the axes of symmetry link inside with outside.

18

In-Between Places

Porches, patios and arcades, which are neither in nor out, connect the inside and the outside. Examples on a smaller scale include the area next to the building under a deep roof overhang, or the outdoor space defined by an interior corner of the building's exterior walls. On an even smaller scale, a deep doorway or window ledge can convey a sense of in-betweenness, linking inside and outside.

Interpenetration

We can relate inside and outside by projecting pieces of the building into the landscape. These extensions of the building's fabric become the links. The wall that continues beyond the interior, reaching out to define exterior space, is an example of this strategy. The drawing at right shows a version from the work of Luis Barragán.

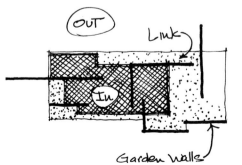

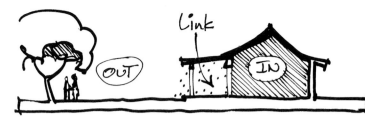

In-between places such as porches and decks link in and out.

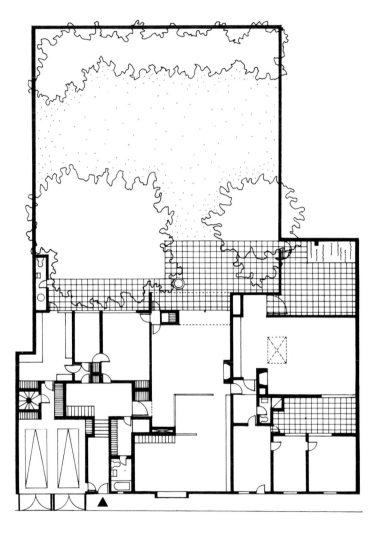

In the house that architect Luis Barragán designed for himself (Tacubaya, Mexico, 1947), the same walls that define the interiors reach out to enclose the garden and patios.

The walls extending beyond the building link it with the surrounding landscape.

19

The indoors and outdoors are linked
by the unexpected placement of
interior elements outside.
(Terrace by William Minschew,
1979, photo © Mark Citret.)

Intermixed Elements

A final technique for relating in and out is to intermix elements, putting exterior elements, such as a tree, inside, or interior elements, such as a fireplace, outside.

3

EXPOSED AND TEMPERED

A building creates a contrast between tempered and exposed spaces. Good buildings allow us to experience both protection and exposure by interrelating them. In this chapter we will look at elements of climatic contrast, and at how to manipulate them in a house so that the occupants can appreciate a full range of experiences. Torrential rain, frigid cold and gale winds may all be enjoyed if there is a sheltered haven nearby — when the house is strong, the storm is good. The goal is to link wetness and dryness, heat and cold, windiness and stillness, quietude and cacophony with a transition area. Examples would include roof overhangs, porches, outdoor rooms, sheltered benches, inglenooks, window seats, enclosed courtyards, interior pools and fountains, garden walls and the sheltering crowns of trees. Let's explore the climatic pairs one by one.

The courtyard in this home is architecturally powerful because it offers the experiential possibilities of many climatic contrasts: wet and dry, warm and cool, sunny and shaded — all linked by the covered patio connecting house and pool. (Photo by Bob Schalkwijk.)

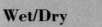

Wet/Dry

In his essay "Personal History — A Soft Spring Night in Shillington" (*The New Yorker*, December 24, 1984, p. 54), John Updike recalled a childhood impression:

> ...the sensation of shelter, of being out of the rain, but just out. I would lean close to the chill windowpane to hear the raindrops ticking on the other side; I would huddle under bushes until the rain penetrated; I loved doorways in a shower. On our side porch, it was my humble job, when it rained, to turn the wicker furniture with its seats to the wall, and in these porous woven caves I would crouch, happy almost to

tears, as the rain drummed on the porch rail and rattled the grape leaves of the arbor and touched my wicker shelter with a mist like the vain assault of an atomic army.

Here, the linking membrane of the glass panes, bushes, doorway and wicker chairs allowed Updike the security of dryness while he experienced the nearness of the rain. Frank Lloyd Wright was being facetious when he said a good building should let the rain leak in a little, but he understood how delightful it is to experience the weather from a safe, dry haven. Indeed, once a building is watertight, the designer should look for ways to reintroduce water as an experiential element.

There are many ways to do this, some of them quite simple. A roof with deep eaves, for example, allows occupants the pleasurable sensation of sitting warm and dry near an open window, hearing and smelling the rain without risk of getting themselves, or the room, wet. From this comfortable and secure position, one can watch the drenching of the nearby landscape, and look out beyond to a bigger world of mist and rain — the overhang forms a boundary between wet and dry. This same overhang enriches the experience of being outside, enjoying a walk in the rain. The availability of the dryness next to the building is enticing, and because the ground under the eaves is dry, walkers may even remove their wet shoes before entering the house. A classic example of a boundary between wet and dry is the porch, a place where the family can gather to experience a summer storm.

A deep covered porch is another way to link wet and dry. Shown is the Saeltzer House in Redding, California (1907), by Bernard Maybeck.

A building's details can enhance the experience of wet and dry. In Japanese houses, the roof drainage system adds visual excitement by allowing water to flow down an exposed chain rather than through a downspout. The water silently flows along the links, reflecting light, then makes a pattern as it pours into a cistern at the base of the chain. In dry weather, the chain is a "memory" of the water flow, and the cistern becomes a still pool. A gargoyle spout is another whimsical approach to keeping walls and walks dry. Water is collected in gutters and funneled out of the creature's mouth over the dry space below. Again, the water runoff is made visible, enriching viewers' understanding of precipitation.

The deep roof overhang creates a link between exposed and tempered. It encourages inhabitants to step out and experience the garden during a rainstorm.

Other examples of linking wet to dry include a courtyard pool edge set at seat height, an open channel of water in a stone courtyard, a hot tub half inside and half outside, an outdoor shower, an indoor pool, a shower with a sliding-glass door to the outside, and a fireplace and couch in the bathroom.

When the bathroom windows are opened, the indoor tub is linked to the outdoor shower and hot tub by a continuous deck level.

This outdoor room is warmed by a fireplace to encourage enjoyment of the crisp outdoor air.

In 1925, Carl Jung built this outdoor room as part of his home in Switzerland. It is deeply dug into the surrounding house and can be warmed by the fireplace even on cool days. The one open side faces the garden and lake beyond. (Photo by Suzanne Crowhurst-Lennard.)

Hot/Cold

Interior air temperature may be so well regulated that it is easy to forget the pleasures of feeling toasty warm or refreshingly cool. One of the reasons we so enjoy trips to the wilderness is that we are able to experience simultaneously the radiant heat of a campfire and the chilly evening air. Some people are rediscovering the thermal pleasure of radiant heating systems in their homes. Like the sun, these systems warm by radiant energy, but they allow the surrounding air temperature to be lowered.

A fireplace in the living room becomes almost a cliche when heating and air conditioning maintain the interior temperature at a constant, "comfortable" level. One way to enliven this deadening evenness is to take the fireplace outdoors, to recreate the campfire situation at home. At its simplest, this can take the form of a fire circle in the backyard, surrounded by benches, where people can gather and talk late into the cool night. Another version of the campfire circle is the outdoor barbecue pit, often built just like a brick fireplace, but including a grate for outdoor cooking. In both these examples, a good contrast exists between the fire's warmth and the air's coolness.

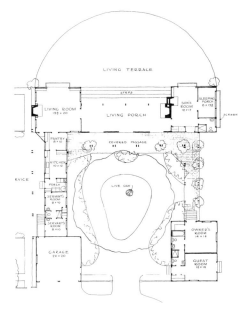

The back wall of the outdoor room in W. W. Wurster's Butler house in Pasatiempo, California (1931-1932), can open to the courtyard to encourage breezes on hot days. On cool days, these doors are closed, and the fire heats the space. (Plan courtesy Richard Peters; photo by Roger Sturtevant.)

An architectural device for linking hot and cold is the outdoor room. This room is at least partially roofed and surrounded on two or three sides by the walls of the house. Its other walls are open to the garden. Adjacent rooms are typically linked to the outdoor room by wide or even double doors to encourage its use. The room itself usually contains a fireplace and is normally large enough to contain a dining table and chairs (with additional lounging chairs, or even sofas); on cold evenings, the fire casts its warmth over the diners. During hot weather, on the other hand, the outdoor room provides a border between the interior coolness of the house and the exterior warmth of the summer day.

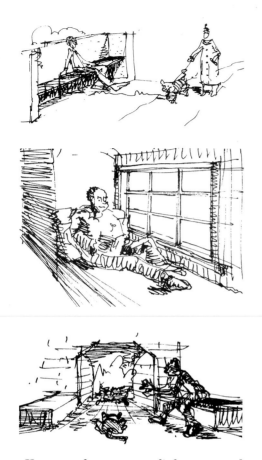

Here are three ways to link warm and cool. The south-facing wall (top) re-radiates the sun's heat; its shape offers shelter from the wind. The window seat (middle) extends an invitation to enjoy the sun from the inside. And the inglenook (above) allows occupants to experience simultaneously the heat of the fire and the colder room beyond.

Three other architectural devices that establish warmth in a cool environment are the south-facing wall, the south-facing window seat and the fireplace inglenook. On a cold, sunny day, a south-facing wall (thermally massive so that it absorbs and stores the radiant heat of the sun) will warm the sitter; if it is concave, the sitter will also be sheltered from the breeze.

The window seat that faces the sun offers a warm spot in an otherwise cool room. The occupant can both receive the warmth of the sun's radiation and enjoy the coolness of the surrounding air.

The fireplace inglenook consists of a fireplace and one or two benches that extend about 6 ft. into the room at right angles to the fireplace sides, all enclosed with walls and a lowered ceiling. It enables users to find just the right amount of heat in a basically cool environment. As such, it links the fire and the cool room. The inglenook may be envisioned as a flaring out of the fireplace into the room, as a subsection of the main room, or as a small room between the fireplace and the main room. Any way you think of it, it allows the sensation of getting into the fire to seek its warmth.

Windblown/Still

The tactile pleasure of feeling the wind blowing over one's body needs to be contrasted with the calmness of still air — an unchanging environment of either extreme becomes tiresome. A partly enclosed courtyard can serve as a boundary between these two extremes. Against the highest surrounding walls the air is nearly motionless; as you move toward the opening, air velocity increases. In addition to wind, sound tends to pass over the top of an enclosed courtyard, so the courtyard is quieter than the surrounding outdoors.

People seek out hilltop building sites because they often offer good views, but the wind is a frequent deterrent to enjoying the outdoors. A courtyard can provide good protection. The house designed by Bernard Maybeck for his son, Wallen, has a courtyard formed on three sides by the walls of the building; the fourth (view) side is bordered by a low wall. Occupants of the courtyard can enjoy both the view and the wind in the treetops beyond, but within feel only gently moving air.

Sleeping outside tests the degree to which the environment has been tempered. The misery of a night spent in a wet sleeping bag in a leaking tent (or in a stifling hot room with inadequate ventilation) isn't quickly forgotten. But it is relatively easy to create a secure, comfortable place that makes outdoor sleeping a real joy: Protect the space with two solid walls and give it a leakproof roof; then allow the occupant to control the degree of openness on the remaining sides. Sleeping porches were a traditional solution, but sadly, they have disappeared from our society's residential vocabulary.

The bed closet is another solution. The closet is filled with the bed, and has windows that open to the outside and sliding panels that separate it from the larger room. This arrangement requires a generous roof overhang to permit sleeping during a rainstorm.

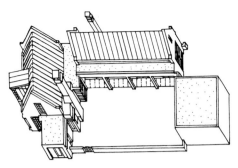

Bernard Maybeck built this house on a windy hill for his son, Wallen, using three sides of the building and a low wall to create a calm, quiet courtyard space in the middle.

This version of a bed closet (designed and built by East Wind, Nevada City, California) uses sliding shoji screens to control the connection to the main room. During a breeze, the rustling tree leaves add to the excitement of being outdoors. (Photo by Jeffrey Westman/Metro Image Group.)

This house, built in 1920 by Bernard Maybeck in Woodside, California, for James F. Fagan, is an essay in how to temper the environment to encourage use of the outdoors. Walls and trellises create spaces for outdoor living and dining, and outdoor sleeping is facilitated with Murphy beds (see the drawing at right).

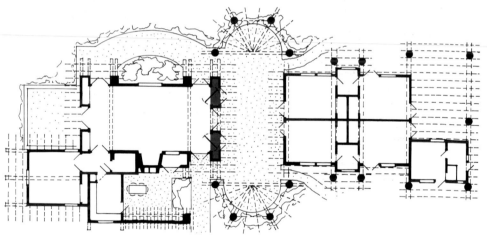

In the Fagan house (1920), Bernard Maybeck provided many options for outdoor eating, dining and sleeping. One of his most interesting concepts was an outdoor Murphy bed. This type of bed stores vertically in a closet; when Maybeck's bed is let down for use, the closet's outside walls open toward the outside, as shown in the drawing above. The sleeper is thus half inside and half outside.

4
UP
AND
DOWN

The up/down dimension of contrast establishes the vertical axis of architecture. We experience this axis through our own bodies, as they extend to the earth below and the sky above. David Ignatow's poem in *Earth Hard* (London: Rapp & Whiting, 1968, p. 62) captures the human experience of up/down.

Earth hard to my heels
bear me up like a child
standing on its mother's belly.
I am a surprised guest to the air.

Up, above

The vertical axis...

Down, below

We define up and down as we orient our bodies to the earth's gravity.

The poem expresses the developmental aspect of up and down. An infant grows into the vertical axis — the baby first lies prone, then sits up, then stands. Each step of the way opens vast new dimensions in the spatial experience of up. Buildings, too, have developed historically from primitive caves and dugouts, essentially down and in kinds of places, to towers that rise up and claim the vertical axis in increasingly complex ways. Similarly, this is how buildings are constructed — from the ground up.

The power of the up/down dimension comes from establishing the contrasting poles of experience within a building. Like Ignatow's poem, a building that rises, a guest of the air, gains strength through experiential contrast with the way it stands on the ground, as it were, with its feet upon its mother's belly.

Creating Up and Down

There are several ways to create the contrasting experiences of up and down in a building. Later in this chapter, we'll discuss ways to link them together.

Ascending/Descending

We experience the effort involved in moving to different levels physically. After providing access and egress for the physically disabled, we create different floor levels simply for the joy of moving about. Just one or two steps suffice to create a distinct separation between two areas (because two steps are more noticeable than one, they won't be tripped over as easily). The contrast between the upper and lower floors of a building will be intensified by unifying all the stairs into a single staircase, enabling occupants to see, understand and experience simultaneously the connection between the upper and lower stories. Steep stairs and ladders increase the sense of up and down, because they intensify the effort of ascent and descent.

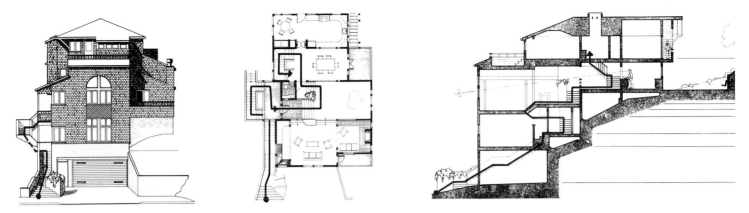

To climb a steep hill, a building becomes a staircase — the retaining walls are its risers and the floors its landings. The Santi residence, designed by Max Jacobson and Murray Silverstein, has eight major landings as it climbs from the dug-in garage to the bedrooms on the highest level.

Stairways create a strong contrast between up and down, at the same time linking the two together. (Lincoln Club, San Francisco, by Gardner Dayley; photo by Roger Sturtevant.)

Changes in ceiling height create an awareness of the up/down dimension. A lower ceiling makes occupants feel taller, whereas a higher ceiling makes them feel shorter.

Typical ceiling height

Lower

Higher

Lowered picture

low plants

Low seating

low or no mantel

Low fireplace

Raised picture

Tall plants

High wainscoting

High mantel

Taller furniture

Lowering a space's horizontal elements will encourage users to sit down. Raising the elements will do the opposite.

Ceiling Height Variety

Residential ceiling heights in the United States are commonly 8 ft. By simply raising the ceiling 6 in. to 12 in., the room can be made to look considerably loftier — and occupants will feel correspondingly shorter. Similarly, lowering the ceiling height by the same amount shrinks the room, and users feel correspondingly taller.

Ceiling height is just one element that designers can manipulate to affect up and down. The horizontal elements of baseboard, wainscoting and fireplace mantel, for example, can be raised to make the room feel shorter and lowered to make the room feel taller. Similarly, if the vertical scale of the room's furniture is interrupted with long, low pieces, the occupants will feel strangely taller, eager to sit down to reduce their relative scale and re-establish normalcy.

Length and Direction of Views

From high up, we see far and can look down upon the landscape. So when trying to create a space that feels high, provide a window with a long view; for an even more powerful effect, lower the windowsill height (or balcony railing) to ensure that residents look down onto something beyond.

The up/down element is strengthened whenever there is a perch or lookout from which users can survey the space below. Such places are often created at stair landings, midway between floors and at interior balconies or catwalks that cross a high space.

Manipulating the Apparent Danger

Our instincts tell us that high spaces are more dangerous — there is always the risk of falling. One way to create the impression of height, therefore, is to increase the apparent danger. Do this by using semi-transparent hand railings (like wood lath), thin balusters of metal (or even tempered glass) or by reducing their height to the minimum required by the building code. Alternatively, the stairs leading up to ever-higher spaces can become steeper and steeper, culminating in a ladder up to the attic. Simply cre-

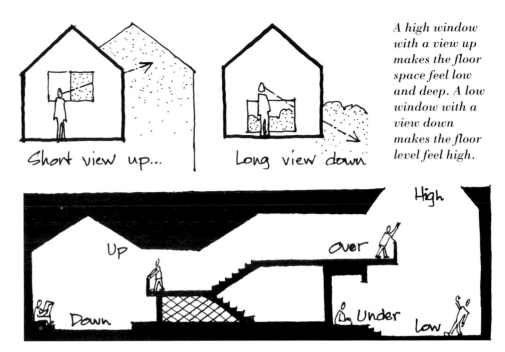

Short view up... Long view down

A high window with a view up makes the floor space feel low and deep. A low window with a view down makes the floor level feel high.

Stair landings enable climbers to look back down over a space below, giving a strong feeling of contrast between up and down.

ating a view into the crown of a tree will allow inhabitants to see the effect of the wind in the swaying branches, making them realize how high up they are.

Semantic Congruity

As you climb a tree, you notice that increased height is accompanied by thinner structure, more light and greater breeziness. By analogy, you can create an increased sense of height with more light and ventilation, and with more delicate framing, trim and decoration. Conversely, you can create an increased sense of depth with less light and breeze, and with a more solid, thicker structure.

33

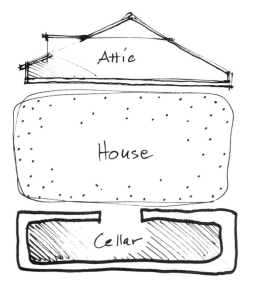

The house links the cool, damp dark of the cellar below with the warmer, drier and lighter attic above.

Linking Up and Down

Here are several techniques for linking up and down.

"Connection" of Separation

Paradoxically, one way of linking two things is to separate and disconnect them intentionally, to make the break between them noticeably sharp and complete. One way to create this kind of nonconnection in a house is to incorporate a traditional cellar and attic—the cool, dark depth of the cellar contrasts with the lofty framed spaces of the attic. But in this age of cheaper building, houses are often built on slabs or with crawl spaces and no cellar; the attic space is also often eliminated. Although it is economical, this type of construction has resulted in a loss of richness in the up/down dimension.

Temporal Connection

You can link up and down in a house by considering how people move through the building when they use it. For example, if all the circulation spaces (halls and foyers) have low ceilings and all the other rooms have high ceilings, occupants will automatically experience a rhythm of up and down as they move through the building. Another example of this type of link is a central patio that is a step or two below the surrounding rooms. Each movement from inside to outside is thus accompanied by an awareness of stepping up or down.

Linking with a Transition

Designers can link up and down by creating a transition between them. This transition can be sharp and focused, or smooth and gradual. But if it is clearly something, it will help occupants form a distinct experience of up and down. For example, connect a high space to a low space with a third, transitional space —perhaps a very high one or one that is very low.

Smooth, continuous transitions gently lead occupants from high to low and back again. Ramps are examples of smooth transitions, as are stairs that are gathered into a single flowing system that is visible as a unity. Or the ceiling in a large space can smoothly curve down toward the walls, creating lower spaces at the edges.

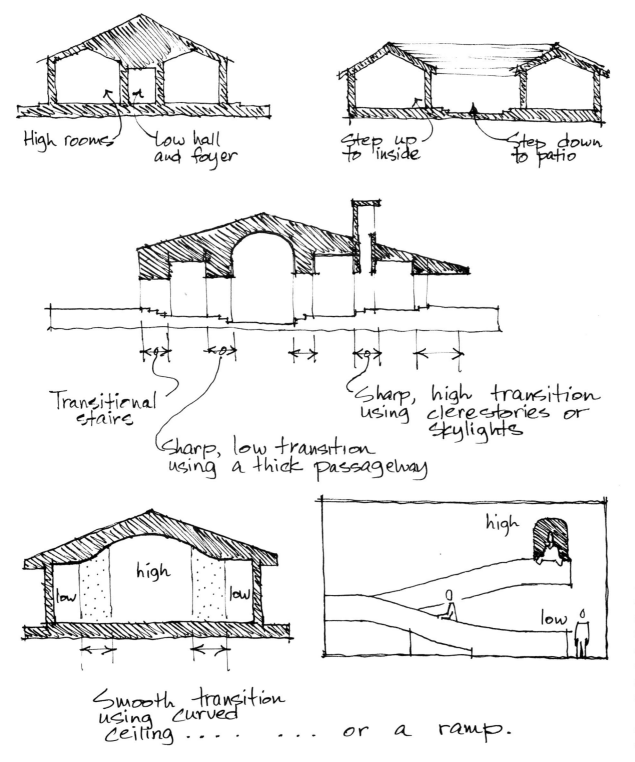

High rooms   Low hall and foyer

Step up to inside   Step down to patio

Transitional stairs

Sharp, low transition using a thick passageway

Sharp, high transition using clerestories or skylights

low   high   low

Smooth transition using curved ceiling . . . .

high

low

. . . or a ramp.

High and low spaces can be linked by transitional spaces that occupants move through as they use the building. The transitions can be smooth or sharp.

35

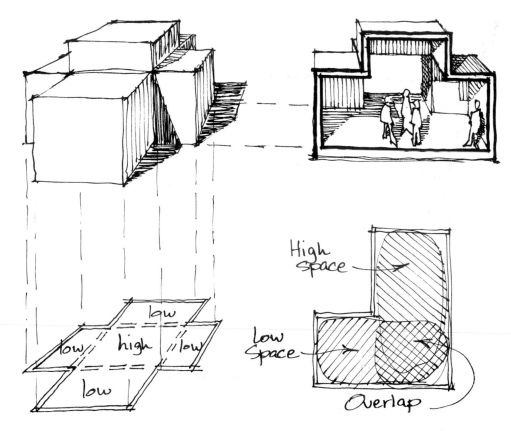

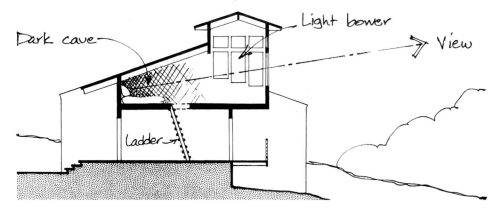

The experience of high and low can be linked if the two spaces interpenetrate and overlap.

This small residential addition embodies both a low cave and a high bower.

Interpenetration

High and low spaces can link by interpenetrating, as shown at left. At the overlap is a space where up and down are experienced simultaneously, where residents can sense the vibrations of each.

Cave Equals Bower

The fundamental opposition of up and down is most directly expressed by two places: a down place (low ceilinged, cavelike, symbolically if not literally dug into the ground) and an up place (higher, lighter, having a view.) But the interpenetration can be so complete that down and up, cave and bower, fuse together in one place. Imagine, for example, a space with a low-ceilinged, dark-paneled nook, two steps down from a larger, higher-ceilinged room that is organized around an extra-large window on axis with a view. The nook is the cave and the high space, with its focus on the view, is the treetop bower. We sought to create this type of experience in a single space in a remodeling project that included an attic study. The space is entered via a steep stair leading up to a low, dark alcove, which opens out on a high space wrapped with tall windows on three sides. The entire space is 12 ft. by 16 ft. in plan.

The Horizontal Scale

Earlier in this chapter we described how a sense of up or down could be created by varying the height of windowsills or ceilings. Here we look at the more general issue of how to link up and down. Up and down can be interrelated by means of a scale, a measuring rod that allows us to see how much distance is involved in getting from one to the other. We cannot very easily experience the height of a sheer 30-story glass-skinned office building without the expression of the floors on its facade to give measure and scale to its height. And we can better experience the height of a room's wall if we can relate it to the horizontal lines of baseboard, windowsills, door jambs and picture rail. Use long, continuous horizontals at different heights to link and relate high and low.

The Structural Link between Up and Down

A final way to discuss the up/down dimension is to look at it from a structural point of view. The ground and foundation are down, the roof and chimney are up; we need to link the two extremes structurally. Begin by examining how the building is linked to the ground. Is it a smooth, flowing connection or a sharp, discontinuous one? Does the

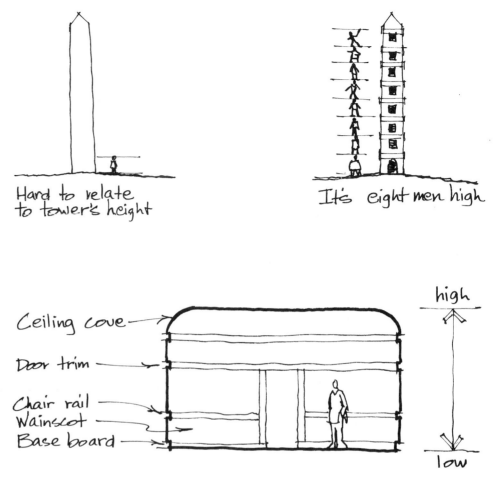

Hard to relate to tower's height

It's eight men high

Ceiling cove
Door trim
Chair rail
Wainscot
Base board

high

low

Horizontal elements enable us to link up and down by giving us a yardstick to estimate the degree of height.

37

Different kinds of boundaries between post and beam —

capital

beam

post

Some emphasize Continuity...

diagonal brace

Hidden pin or bolt

.. others discontinuity.

The building above is linked to the ground below by various kinds of footings, just as the beams above are linked to the posts below by various kinds of connections.

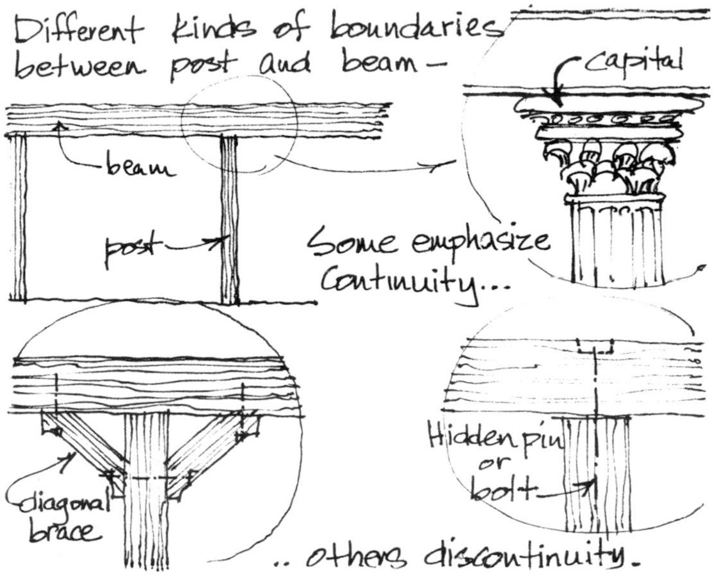

Steel half I-beams on concrete piers form a discontinuous effect as do poles extending through air and water into the ground. Buildings that grow out of the ground have a continuous effect.

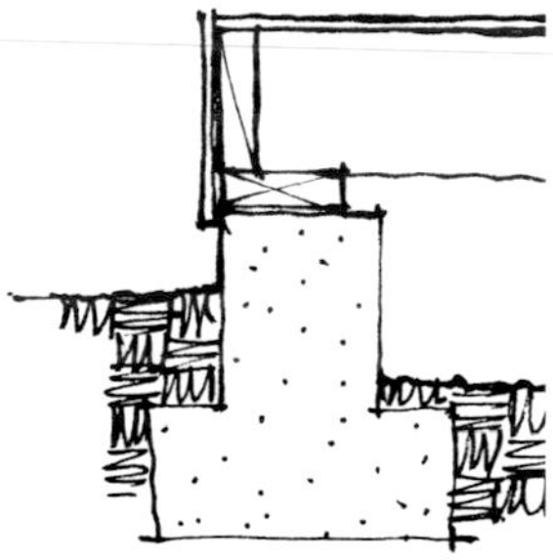

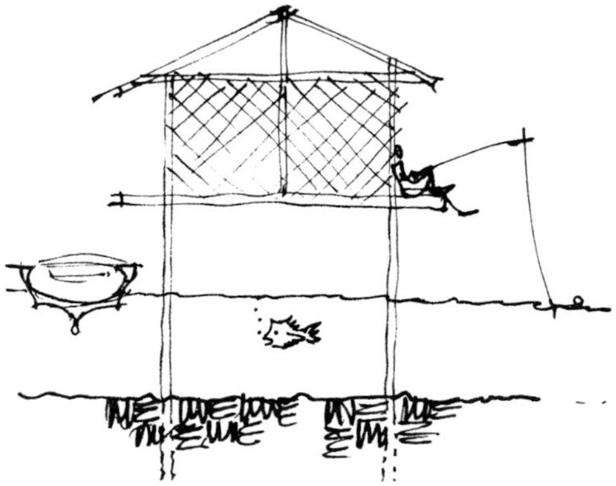

connection express the up of the building and the down of the ground? Typical links between the building and the ground are shown at left.

Look at some of the more detailed ways that the structure of the building relates up and down. For example, at any floor the structure above our heads is typically borne by joists, and this load is transferred (or linked) to the underlying floor by walls and beams or columns. These links can be smooth or discontinuous, but they must be there in some form or the building will collapse. The building can make us aware that there is a load up there and a supporting ground down there; this is done through the design of the linking structure.

At an even smaller scale, look at the way in which the upper loads within the beam are carried down into an underlying post or column via a link between the two, a joint that can be infinitely varied, but which has the potential capacity of expressing the flow of load from up to down.

5

SOMETHING AND NOTHING

Thirty spokes
share one hub.
Adapt the nothing therein to the purpose in hand,
and you will have the use of the cart.
Knead clay in order to make a vessel. Adapt the nothing
therein to the purpose in hand, and you will have the use
of the vessel.
Cut out doors and windows in order to make a room. Adapt
the nothing therein to the purpose in hand, and you will
have use of the room.
Thus what we gain is Something, yet it is by virtue of
Nothing that it can be put to use.   —*Lao Tzu*

Henry Moore's Recumbent Figure *gains its strength from the play of solid, earthy, fleshy substance and the open, inviting space within it. (Tate Gallery, London/Art Resource, N. Y.)*

Buildings consist of an interplay between something — a physical material, object or area of information — and nothing — the emptiness and space in between. Together they define shape and meaning.

Imagine all the things that comprise a house — the materials of construction and the objects that will later fill it — transported to a site on a huge truck. The pile of stuff is considerably smaller than the eventual house. Clearly, the finished house contains lots of empty space — lots of nothingness. When the truck arrives at the site, the house builder's job is to sort the load into meaningful piles, separated from one another by areas of nothingness, and then to interrelate and link these piles to one another in such a way as to produce a finished house.

A building, like a sculpture, consists of solid and void, of something and nothing. In sculptor Henry Moore's *Recumbent Figure*, the stone feels fuller by contrast with the emptiness, and the holes and cavities feel emptier by contrast with the dense stone. The whole form is shaped by this sharp play of contrast. Moore's forms are powerful and appealing because they resemble us. We, too, are made of the interplay of something and nothing, both physically and psychologically, and the sculpture speaks to us about the human condition.

Creating Something/Nothing

The "something" of architecture is a building's density of mass, form and decoration. "Nothingness" is the diffuseness or absence of these elements.

Our understanding of fullness involves the appearance of solidity (opacity, density), the fact of solidity (permanence, heaviness) and structural solidity (our sense of the way in which the object transfers its loads to the earth).

The appearance of architectural solidity is established by the shape of a building and the relative opacity of its walls. Buildings that cascade down from high points like miniature mountains seem the most substantial of all. Even though a tall, thin, steel-frame structure might be more permanent than a mountain-shaped wood-frame building, it is clear that the mountain form better expresses solidity.

The composition of walls and the openings in them also help establish a feeling of solidity. Walls having few small openings, which appear as opaque planes, establish solidity. This is reinforced if the openings reveal the walls to be unexpectedly thick and composed of materials that require thickness for structural integrity. The walls may not, in fact, be thick, but they can be designed to create the impression of depth and substance by enclosing voids or including other elements in the apparent thickness of the wall. By contrast, installing aluminum sliding-glass doors and windows flush with the exterior surface emphasizes the thinness of the standard framed wall.

To appear more solid, buildings can be shaped like miniature mountains, whose forms rest in the gentle slope achieved after years of slow erosion and settlement—the 'angle of repose.'

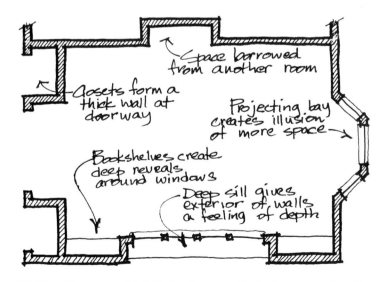

Walls will appear thick if the doors and windows are placed to create a deep recess. The spaces between can be used for storage or display. To create a niche, space can be borrowed from adjoining rooms.

Despite its small scale and lightweight shell, the Taylor house in Inverness, California (designed by the authors), gains a sense of permanence and solidity from the exposed heavy timber frame. (Photo by Susan Felter.)

The fact of solidity is established by the use of dense, heavy, permanent materials. Create this side of the contrast by using stone, masonry, thick stucco and heavy wooden timbers. Touching these materials while moving through the building, feeling the unyielding floors and walls and hearing sound bouncing off the solid surfaces all help create a feel for the solidity of a building.

Finally, the sense that something is substantial is confirmed by its connection to the ground. In general, a building will look more substantial if it is connected to the ground by a broad, spreading base or footing. The Moore sculpture rests on a solid concrete pedestal atop a solid slab. The design of classical buildings made of masonry materials requires a particular architectural order, which includes a base as well as a capital.

The foundation of the Taylor house has a broad, sloping base, creating a strong tie to the ground and expressing the substantial quality of the building above. (Photo by Susan Felter.)

42

The lightweight, airy quality of the trusses in the Anderson studio in Denver, Colorado (designed by the authors), balances the enclosed feeling created by the steep roof form.

To balance the feeling of density and mass in a house, create emptiness by incorporating transparency, lightness and fragility. Use forms that are skeletal, like open roof trusses (see the photo above), delicate filigree or open trellises and latticework; these structures have been lightened by the removal of all unnecessary material. The feeling of emptiness can also be created by using a smooth, continuous material that mirrors the space rather than calling attention to itself. The interior of a masonry dome or a vault with relatively few windows can become a light, airy bubble if the interior skin is smooth and white.

The quality of nothingness can also be achieved with flexible materials that yield to the touch, such as canvas, lath and paper. A gravel path, for example, shifts slightly underfoot, sounding a note of fragility and freedom. Tent structures are composed of flexible materials stretched into forms — beautiful bubbles of nothing. In climates where outdoor living is possible, such structures can be integrated with permanent buildings.

The delicate quality of the light inside a tent becomes mysterious and compelling when opaque patterns on the surface mingle with the shadows of branches from the trees above. (Photo by Slobodan Dan Paich.)

43

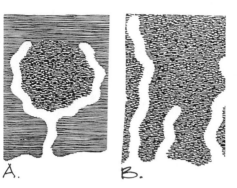

Thus far we have emphasized the role of three-dimensional mass in creating fullness in architecture, but we need to remember the role of two-dimensional shapes. The Gestalt principles of good form show that the perceived thingness of an object is strongly affected by its shape. A shape that is closed is perceived as more of a thing than a freeform open shape (which is perceived as background). And the perceived thingness of an element can be intensified by giving the object axes of symmetry.

The surfaces of architecture can also display various areas of fullness and emptiness. Surface mass is conveyed by the decoration, density and weight of the visual material — the boldness of line. Nothingness is felt in empty space, delicate tones and uniformly shaded areas with no sudden discontinuities.

Linking Something/Nothing

Up to now we have discussed something and nothing as isolated experiences, but the power of this element lies in the way the contrasting halves are brought together. On pp. 45-48 are several ways to relate these contrasting elements.

The smooth emptiness of the Assyrian bull's flanks is contrasted with the surface richness and fullness of the wings and plaited hair. (Louvre, Paris.)

The massiveness of the half-wall and fireplace contrasts with the insubstantiality of the hanging awning overhead. Associated contrasts of light/dark, in/out and exposed/tempered are offered in this house by artist/architect William Minschew. (Photo © Mark Citret.)

Something in a Field of Nothing

Set a full, rich, massive object in a generous field of emptiness:

A Japanese rock garden allows viewers to see the richness of rocks by placing them in an expanse of precisely raked sand.

Put a single picture on a perfectly blank, clean wall surface to encourage new appreciation.

Eliminate unnecessary clutter so that the fullness of select objects can be enjoyed.

The view to the ocean gains new power when shaped by the space between two very solid forms. At Louis Kahn's Salk Biology Center, another link between solid and void is the narrow channel of water cutting through the solid concrete on its path toward the ocean.

Frank Lloyd Wright's Fallingwater gains spatial excitement from the interplay of massive, solid structural elements and airy open spaces. (Drawing by Melissa Harris.)

Shape Emptiness with Something

Use mass to shape the empty space. Some architects pursue this with all the purity of Henry Moore. For example, when designing the Salk Biology Center in La Jolla, California, Louis Kahn split a pair of scientific laboratories with an austere court, a space of infinite emptiness that reaches out toward the Pacific Ocean.

This technique of using the building mass to give thinglike shape to enclosed or surrounding spaces is one of the most powerful tools of the architect. It enables courtyards to feel roomlike and rooms to feel whole and settled; spaces that have understandable forms encourage occupants to relax — the rooms don't demand their attention. Something and nothing coexist to make form; each has a shape for which the other is ground. This fact is a major aesthetic principle in architecture, graphics and music.

Something and Nothing Interpenetrate

Frank Lloyd Wright was often photographed with his hands clasped, fingers intertwined, as he talked about the need for spaces to interpenetrate. His house for the Kaufmann family, Fallingwater, shown in the drawing at left, is perhaps the

46

most famous house built in the 20th century. It is a wonderful example of the interpenetration of solid, massive building elements and massless, empty spatial elements.

The Something/Nothing Gradient

Squeeze out a blob of paint on a wet sheet of paper, and streak it across with your finger. The color at first is intense, but at the end of the streak it's completely faded out. This gradient of something/nothing is satisfying because it allows viewers to contact both ends of the spectrum simultaneously.

The structural logic of buildings suggests that the base, which carries the greatest load, must be heavy, but that the supporting elements should become lighter as the building becomes higher and less mass is carried above. Seeing forms that reflect this intuitive understanding confirms our structural awareness. As Gothic cathedrals were built taller and taller, it became necessary to lighten the upper portions and strengthen and thicken the lower portions, forming a gradient of mass. It is satisfying to see flags and flimsy awnings waving in the breeze at the tops of buildings and to see strong, massive foundations at their bases. The lightness at the top helps us to see the weight at the bottom.

Gothic cathedrals were composed of high spaces shaped to reflect the religious aspirations of their builders. Their massive columns, thick walls and flying buttresses were dictated by structural necessity. Together they appeal to both the spirit and the mind. (Drawing by Forrest Wilson.)

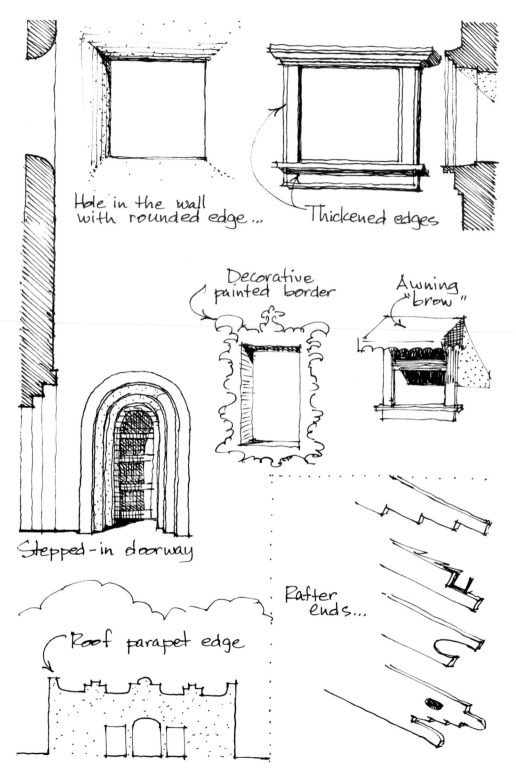

Hole in the wall with rounded edge...

Thickened edges

Decorative painted border

Awning "brow"

Stepped-in doorway

Rafter ends...

Roof parapet edge

Create a Border between Something and Nothing

A classic way to unite two things is with a border. The material of a bowl or cup, for example, has only one topological discontinuity—at its edge. The vessel is structurally weak at this discontinuity and is sometimes thickened there to form a lip—the border between something and nothing. The same thickened edge is at the openings of doors and windows. Some other examples include the borders of rug edges (the fringe), the decorated edge of a parapet roof and the fancy cuts at rafter ends, put there just for fun.

Borders at the edges link contrasting building features.

6

LIGHT
AND
DARK

The contrast between light and dark allows us to see form. Our eyes search for contrasts in light quality, focusing on the linking borders between them. In a constant, uniform field of light, we see nothing.

We schedule our lives around the cyclical pattern of day and night, light and dark. Yet in each phase of the cycle there is an integration of the opposite — the night is brightened by the stars and the moon; daylight is relieved by shadows, which lengthen as darkness approaches. At the boundaries between light and dark, sunrise and sunset provide the essential links, brilliant elements that mark the transition between day and night. Houses, too, require an integration of light and dark, and the presence of color or pattern as the border, or event, between them.

Creating Light and Dark

We are attracted to places that are defined by a contrast in light level. When we choose an interior place to sit, it is almost always in the light — at a window, near a fire or beside a candle or lamp. On the other hand, when outdoors and in bright sun, we tend to seek the dappled light beneath an umbrella, tree or porch roof.

In dark spaces, create contrast by introducing light from concentrated sources — from a single large window or overhead skylight. The shaft of direct light will move around the room with the sun, intensifying the sense of the passing day. In the evening, intensify the gathering power of the fireplace by lighting only that area, dimming the room's other lighting. You may also create contrast between light and dark by using clustered artificial lights.

Similarly, consider how to create shadows within very light places. Shadows define forms three-dimensionally and prevent the disorientation that comes with perceiving no depth or shape, only the light in a uniformly lit room. Shadows also create new and unpredictable shapes, bringing interest and variety to a surface. And like moving shafts of light, they contribute to the sense of passing time.

The play of shadow and light adds richness and texture to the simple white adobe patio of Georgia O'Keefe's New Mexico home. (Photo by Balthazar Korab Ltd.)

Using the light of a window or a desk lamp to define a bright work area makes it easier to direct attention to the task at hand.

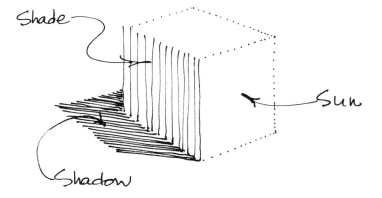

An object's form is defined by the play of light across it and by the location of light and shade. Additional information about both the object and the source of light can be gained from the shadow.

The moving shadow helps to link the casting and receiving surfaces to each other, to define shapes and surfaces and to record the passing of time. (Photo by Slobodan Dan Paich.)

The intricate trellis over the courtyard of Abdel Wahed El-Wakil's Sulaiman Palace in Saudi Arabia fragments the intense sunlight into intricate geometric patterns. (Photo by Abdel Wahed El-Wakil.)

Linking Light and Dark

At the boundary of light and dark, it is important to introduce an element that links the two together. This new element, which possesses a wholeness and beauty of its own, moderates and tempers the brightness contrast.

Filtering and Controlling Sunlight

Eyelashes shade our eyes from overhead light and moderate the difference between bright light and total shade. When the sun is very bright, we add additional layers of protection: sunglasses, a visor or a hat with a broad brim.

A similar approach to the control of natural light is needed in the design of homes and gardens. Providing an overhead screen will filter the light as eyelashes do. In outdoor settings, the screen may be trees or trellises, which provide dappled shade. Indoors, windows that are broken into small panes, protected by filigreed latticework or shaded by the branches of a tree achieve this effect — the sunlight is broken into small but brilliant fragments.

Greater protection can be added with shadecloth or canvas awnings, translucent roofing or filmy curtains; occupants will still experience the light, but with diminished intensity. For maximum protection, build visors of solid materials overhead to create dense shade. Extended eaves, roofed porches and deeply inset windows create a shadowy space from which to look out into the light.

The grapevines growing on the trellis of the Sailer house, designed by the authors, offer seasonal shade; in summer, cool filtered light is admitted, while in winter, patterned sunlight flows through the windows.

Interior Glare and Sparkle

Introducing light into a room from a single window or skylight can create high contrast between light and dark. But it can also cause painful glare. Prevent glare by better linking the light to dark, perhaps by creating an intermediate border with one of the following: a deep window reveal that flares out toward the room, reflecting an intermediate level of light; a rounded sill and jamb, which create a smooth transition between light and dark; very light-colored interior window trim; or, to temper the sharp contrast between light and dark, a second light source on another wall.

The dining room of the Sailer house has several light sources. Outdoor light is introduced through a window seat. This is balanced by general artificial lighting and by a centered recessed cove overhead, illuminated by hidden fluorescent tubes wrapped with brown paper to create a warmer-color light.

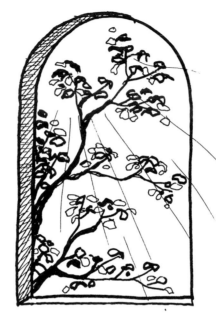

Tiny white Christmas-tree lights spread throughout a tree reveal the tree's form even in darkness, giving it a magical, sparkling quality. A similar effect occurs when we look through a tree toward the sunlight beyond. The pattern of leaves and branches breaks up the sunlight into small, brilliant fragments — we can look directly into the light and enjoy its brightness because it is diffused.

A final glare-eliminating technique requires breaking up the source of light into many smaller sources. A large window can be broken into many smaller panes, in the style of a stained-glass window, for example. Or in artificial lighting, a few single sources can be replaced with additional smaller ones. For example, a chandelier of tiny lights will create a pleasant, lively effect called sparkle. Or a recessed lighting cove concealing several bulbs casting bounced light will create a subtle glowing effect.

Sequence of Light and Dark

As occupants move through a building, they will feel the contrast between light and dark more intensely if they experience a rhythmic sequence of light/dark/light/dark. This alternation of light and dark can be created by using skylights at important hall junctions, by installing a regular pattern of ceiling lights along the length of a hall or by collecting windows into recognizable groups.

The high windows in the light towers at each end of the hallway of the Hobert house, designed by the authors, create a bright spot to move toward.

The color wheel places complementary (or contrasting) colors opposite each other, while adjacent colors are related by a common tone.

The blue shutters and cool white walls typically found on the Greek island of Hydra provide welcome contrast to the hot Mediterranean sun.

Houses in the small town of Dragør, Denmark, are painted warm yellow, which combines with red tile roofs and soft brown thatch to create a sense of warmth in this cool climate. (Photo by Gary Coates.)

The spectrum of visible light can be represented as a color wheel. Complementary colors, which lie opposite each other on the wheel, contrast intensely with each other. Natural sunlight contains the full spectrum of color, incorporating all the complementary colors.

Perhaps our bodies require a balance of the warm and cool colors that compose white light. If so, it explains why sunlight contributes so much to well-being and balance. Fluorescent light is not balanced — it is deficient in the warm, red portion of the spectrum — and its exclusive use can lead to a tired, irritable mood. It needs to be balanced with warmer light from incandescent sources.

The need for balance in color is illustrated by the traditional colors used for buildings in different climates. Mediterranean structures are whitewashed, their doors and shutters often accented with intense blues or greens. The long summer and the high sun combine to create an environment in which the light is bright and warm — the white walls reflect the sun while the cool-colored accents provide contrast and relief. On the other hand, buildings in the cold Scandinavian climate are typically made of brick or wood colored in warm tones and accented with reds and oranges. Both these materials absorb the limited sunlight and balance the cooler colors of the landscape.

In general, using complementary colors will produce a stimulating effect. But unless these colors are linked, they may fight each other —if you place a very saturated red next to a very saturated green, you'll notice a visual vibration at the border, which can be unpleasant in a building. There are at least five ways to link complementary colors, techniques that allow the colors to retain the energy of contrast while producing a balanced interaction. We will describe each method using green and red, although the principles would be the same for violet and yellow, or orange and blue.

A. Scatter a small amount of green throughout a field of red. A kind of energized balance will result between the dominant red and the recessive green.

B. Dilute (or desaturate) the green with white. The pale green and the strong red will coexist comfortably.

C. Mix the colors a little, adding a little green to the red and vice versa, and the colors will begin to link. (This could, of course, eventually lead to a single muddy color in the middle, which is not what we are talking about.)

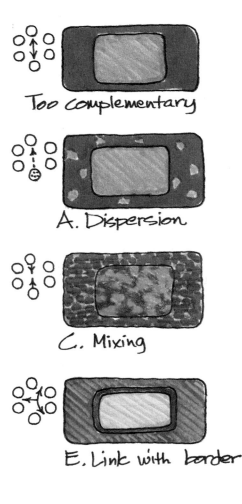

D. Push the contrasting colors toward each other by adding a little of a third color to each. For example, add a little yellow-orange to both the red and green. The resulting orange-red and yellow-green will relate well to each other.

E. Further link these colors by creating a bold, contrasting border between them. For example, you could link the orange-red and the yellow-green with a border of blue-violet, which will contrast equally with each of them.

This drawing shows the clash of complementary and neighboring colors and the harmony of the following kinds of links: (A) dispersion of one member; (B) desaturation of one member; (C) mixing, or 'walking toward each other;' (D) inflection toward each other by mixing in a common third color; and (E) sharing a border of a third color.

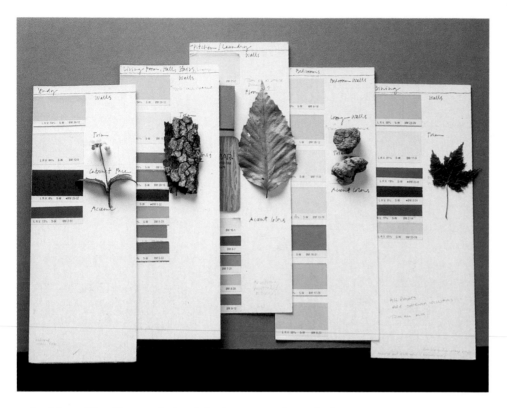

Architect Kim Tanzer derived the interior colors of a house from the surrounding natural colors of leaves, twigs and rocks. Tanzer says, 'We followed the colors found on the underside of a new maple leaf for the dining-room palette, with muted grey-green walls, dusty white trim and burgundy accents.' The contrasting, complementary red and green are linked by desaturating the green and adding blue to the red. (Photo © Jerry Markatos.)

Because the colors of buildings are not usually arbitrary, these techniques will typically be mixed and combined to achieve the desired results. The challenge is to coordinate the built-in color limitations and potentials of the materials being used. The building should also attempt to contrast with the predominant set of colors of the surrounding landscape.

A Place in between Light and Dark

Finally, try to link light and dark by creating a special place in between, where both can be experienced simultaneously. Link the darker indoors to the lighter outdoors with a window seat, a bay window or a greenhouse. Link the brighter outdoors to the cooler, darker indoors with a porch, a shaded patio or even a generous roof overhang.

7

ORDER AND MYSTERY

Order is essential to our understanding of the world; without it we could not process information, formulate plans, make decisions or compare possibilities. The existence of a natural order — of a predictable cycle of day and night, seasonal changes and life cycles — provides a structure within which we can experience growth. The certainty of a set of predictable events creates the freedom to make choices and experience their impact, knowing that life on the grand scale will continue unimpeded. Our basic understanding of the larger order of the universe and our place within it allows us to accept the apparent randomness of the daily flow of events.

The truly memorable happenings in our lives are often those that are major departures from the familiar order: births, marriages and deaths; hurricanes, earthquakes and eclipses. Because they are not part of the usual pattern, these events take on a larger-than-life quality, leading us to examine, question and appreciate our daily experiences.

Creating Order and Mystery

In our houses, as in our lives, we seek a basic underlying order. There must be structural order for a building to withstand the forces of gravity, weather and movement. Functional order allows the building to respond to the needs and schedules of its occupants. And formal order organizes the spaces geometrically, making the building intelligible to its users. It is only within the framework of order in a house that occupants can pleasurably experience the unexpected, the mysterious. And yet it is the unpredictable places that have the greatest potential to command attention and excite curiosity.

Geometrical Order/Mystery

There are several kinds of geometrical descriptions encountered in architecture — symmetry, progression, packings and fractal geometry. Geometrical symmetries (radial, bilateral and multilateral) all serve to reduce the complexity of the system and to introduce order, a sense of control. But these symmetries can become deadening unless balanced and contrasted with asymmetries. Symmetry says that everything is the same on both sides of the axes; asymmetry says that things are different. Asymmetries can arise from a response to the specifics of a site, the path of the sun or wind (like the directional wind flap on the otherwise radially symmetrical tepee), from functional needs or simply from the aesthetic desire to create them (as in Japanese gardening, where symmetry is considered unnatural).

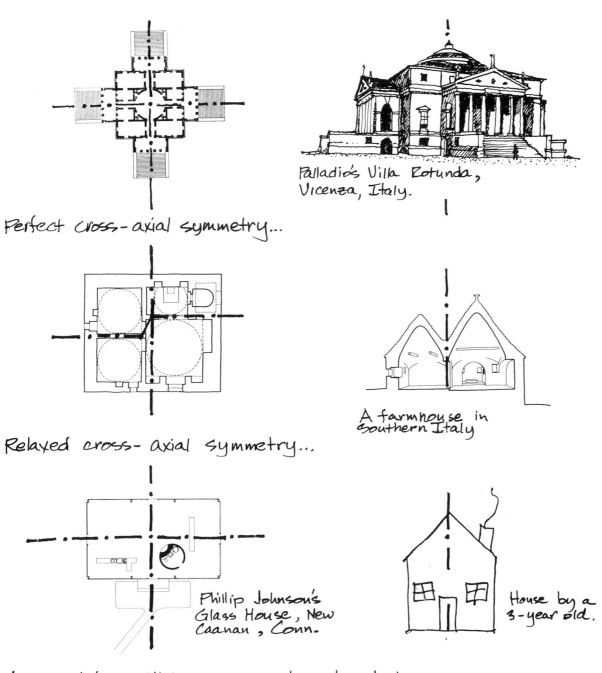

Perfect cross-axial symmetry...

Palladio's Villa Rotunda, Vicenza, Italy.

Relaxed cross-axial symmetry...

A farmhouse in Southern Italy

Phillip Johnson's Glass House, New Caanan, Conn.

House by a 3-year old.

Asymmetries within a symmetrical whole.

Symmetry creates strong, formal order. When symmetries are broken but still recognizable, they suggest mysterious, unpredictable forces with the power to alter the rules of order.

61

Simple rhythms of equally spaced windows, columns or decorations are examples of geometrical progressions. More complex are those typified by spiral forms, like the arrangement of seeds in a pine cone. Le Corbusier's Modulor system of proportioning is based in part upon the progression 1,2,3,5,8,13,21..., in which each number is the sum of the two previous ones. Le Corbusier proposed his Modulor as an ordering system based upon the proportions of the human body and on mathematics. He used the system in many projects, most notably in his housing project at Marseilles, where the shape of all of the plans, sections and elevations is derived from it.

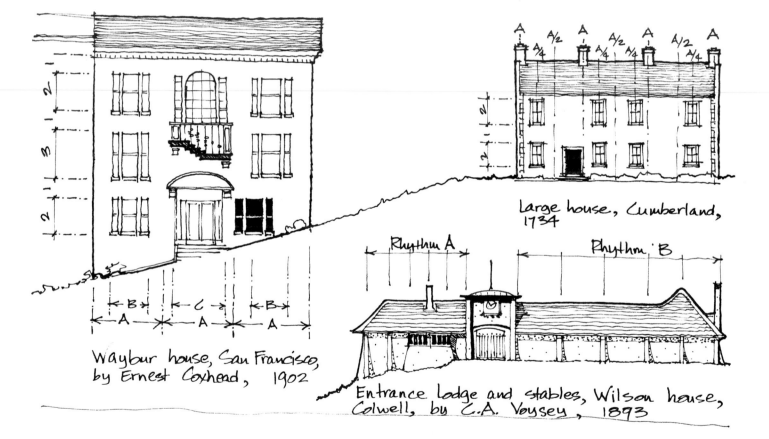

Waybur house, San Francisco, by Ernest Coxhead, 1902

Large house, Cumberland, 1734

Entrance lodge and stables, Wilson house, Colwell, by C.A. Voysey, 1893

Such orderly progressions can be contrasted with disorderly arhythmic occurrences. When both are incorporated into a building, our attention will be drawn to where they interact with each other. Knowing this, architects will often introduce an arhythmic element into an otherwise rhythmic composition simply to emphasize the importance of that part of the building.

Geometrical packings are created when a volume or plane is completely filled, or packed, with one or more regular shapes. Geometrical packings are encountered in two-dimensional patterns as well as in three-dimensional organizations of volumes. Such geometries are beautiful in their inevitability and rationality, but in architectural forms they need to be balanced by the disorder of gaps in the packing or they can be harsh and oppressive. Packing disorder is created by not fitting the pieces as tightly together as possible, by creating usable spaces between. Sometimes packing disorder is created unwittingly, as when two unrelated grids collide (like street systems), or when the open space between buildings gets squeezed down through many years of expansion and rebuilding. We need both — the order of well-packed spaces for spatial efficiency, and the disorder of interstitial spaces that occurs in response to local forces, thereby offering variety and opportunity.

The simple order of this Shaker sewing desk, based on a vertical bilateral symmetry and a horizontal three-two progression, is mysteriously interrupted by the apparent functional need to create a bank of side drawers.

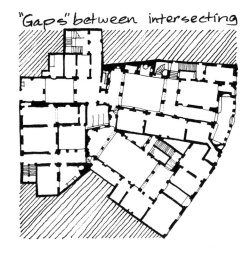

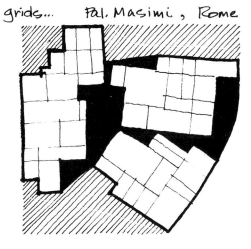

The order of strict geometric packing can be enlivened by irregular shapes or gaps in the packing.

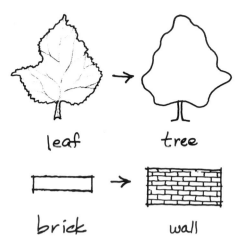

leaf → tree

brick → wall

In fractal geometry, order is generated by a rough equivalence in form between parts and whole. The surprise occurs when the part is 'bent' to create areas of novelty within the overall order.

..the surprise of the arch

Functional Order/Ambiguity

Buildings can make clear functional distinctions, such as public/private, service/serviced or wet/dry. But they can also create fuzzy zones of disorder where clear distinctions break down. This occurs, for example, when we recognize that the kitchen is also a social space—it may be the place where kids do homework and adults keep their files and pay bills; and when we recognize that a bedroom may also be the best place to lounge with friends or grow plants.

Display cooking in a restaurant, for example, allows the dining space to be linked to the cooking space with wonderful smells, sights and sounds. Counter dining or an open kitchen area offers neither total functional separation nor total functional integration and can nicely connect the pleasures of cooking with eating.

In the design of a house, first organize clear and distinct functional areas, then soften and enrich the order with ambiguity. Reconnect the areas with interior windows and openings to hallways. Or put the areas at different ends of the same room, or allow them to share an interior courtyard.

Fractal geometry refers to the geometric equivalency between the parts and the whole that occurs naturally in minerals and organisms. It is an old idea—Goethe noted that the shape of a whole tree was the same as one of its leaves. In building, one could imply that a structure of bricks should have the overall shape of a brick, as it roughly does in a brick wall. But such order needs to be countered with an occasional willingness to "bend" the materials, to show that they can do what might, at first, be surprising. In the middle of the regularity of a brick wall, for example, the bricks can leap up and become an arch.

Permanence/Change

The successful house responds to the dual needs for permanence and change. Some parts of the building will be unchanging — the foundation and basic structure (we hope), the overall scheme of parking, entry and stairs and the arrangement of the most formal rooms. Other parts will be in relative flux, like the seasonal garden, the kitchen, the multi-purpose room, a display niche or canvas awnings and waving curtains. You can create more awareness of the permanent elements by exposing them, making them thicker, heavier and more geometrically regular and predictable. Similarly, provoke awareness of the temporal elements by exposing them, making them thinner and lighter, and more geometrically irregular.

Now try to link the contrasts: Make a special, permanent niche to contain a changing display of flowers or other natural objects. In this way, a knot garden is a regular geometric arrangement of seasonal plants. Those elements of the house that have relatively short lives can be temporarily attached to the larger structure so clearly and visibly that occupants are encouraged to replace them (tatami mats, awnings attached with grommets or vulnerable trim attached with screws instead of nails). Create places that

A permanent display niche is incomplete without a changing display. This one is in the Kuperman house, designed by the authors.

invite their users to freshen and renew them periodically. The random renewal of such places, within a relatively unchanging framework of permanence, can be a lovely embodiment of this dimension of contrast — the mystery is the surprising power of a change in detail when set off against an overall order.

Hand Work/Machine Work

The workmanship required for the construction of a house involves a balance between machine work and hand work, between control and freedom. Factory-produced components (such as panels of plywood and corrugated metal, or modular cabinetry) require very controlled workmanship; site-built assemblies (such as stucco and plaster walls) allow less rigid control and the possibility of freer workmanship.

The workmanship of houses today tends to overemphasize the control of the machine and underemphasize the freedom of the hand, mainly because of the standardized dimensions of the components. We sometimes react to this dominance of the machine by deliberately rusticating materials (sandblasting, distressing or antiquing wood, blowtorching stone, buying fake used bricks), but this is not often satisfactory.

A better approach is to contrast differing levels of machine work and hand work, each of honest, direct and natural workmanship. For example, you might contrast hand-textured stucco work with machine-planed wood. The stucco shows the hand and trowel of the plasterer; the wood shows the machine precision of the planer. Handmade tiles set rhythmically into a field of factory-made tiles create a similar effect. In general, it is a mistake to try to make handwork look like machine work, and vice versa.

The Penn house, designed by the authors (see pp. 114-122), features a hand-crafted stair of wood and tile that contrasts boldly with the machine-crafted walls of aluminum and glass that surround it.

8

THE CONTRASTING WHOLE

In this first section of the book, we have attempted to develop a direct way of approaching the analysis and design of buildings. To the question "What makes a good building?" we answered that, at each level of scale, the building must be energized with contrasting elements, which interlock to form a contrasting whole. If the building, then, is to have some part or element that feels strongly inside, it must be linked with another part or element that feels relatively outside, and so on.

In the last six chapters, we have explored the dimensions of contrast that are most germane to building design. Now we will pull these separate ideas together to create a summary of the theoretical good house.

The main concept of this chapter is that the various dimensions of contrast are themselves interrelated and linked into an integrated whole. In Chapters 2 through 7, the dimensions of environmental contrast were presented as independent variables, as if in/out could be manipulated independently from exposed/tempered or light/dark. But in fact the various dimensions are linked to one another: We intuitively sense, for example, that up is linked to light and down is linked to dark. These built-in associations between the dimensions are indications that environmental experience is not just a collection of separate, isolated impressions, but is organized instead into a larger, more unified structure. Perhaps there is a single archetypal image of "house," and any one particular house is measured or experienced in relation to this ideal. But let us first look at how these various dimensions of contrast connect to each other.

House and Site

Many of the links between the dimensions of contrast are rooted in observations of the larger environment into which buildings are placed. Nature presents landscapes that have typical arrays of associated qualities. For example, we expect a forest to offer a cluster of qualities including damp, dark, cool and tempered. Similarly, desert qualities include dry, hot, glaringly bright and exposed. Naturally occurring linkages such as these have become part of our general understanding of how the world is put together.

Buildings can take on these coherent clusters of qualities in several ways. First, the physical building may in fact create a micro-environment that closely corresponds to a naturally occurring one. An example would be a cellar, which, like a cave, is low, dark and damp, with an even, cool temperature.

Second, the design may attempt to imitate some aspect of nature, for example, to capture a cave-like feeling in a family room or study. In such a case, it would be appropriate to design a step down to the room rather than up, to lower the light level relative to the surrounding spaces and to introduce rougher, darker textures into the fabric of the room — all for the effect of imitating a cavelike space.

Third, instead of imitating nature, a house may set itself up in partial opposition to the natural characteristics of the site to correct some of its perceived deficiencies. A building in the arid, untempered climate of the desert will therefore try to counteract that cluster of characteristics. Traditionally, desert houses are built of thick, massive earthen materials to temper the difference between hot days and chilly nights. Windows and doors are minimal to exclude the glare of the sun. An attempt is made to increase interior humidity by passing air over an interior cistern or pool of water. The hot, dry, exposed characteristics of the site are opposed and contrasted by the building's humid, tempering solidity.

House and Materials

The plans for a house consist of paper and pencil lines, measurements and geometries, all expressing abstract concepts, aspirations and feelings. But the design will eventually be built in the physical world with real materials. All of the contrasting qualities that are indicated on paper with drawings and notes will eventually be expressed by wood and stone, wallboard and paint. How will the design be influenced by these materials?

One obvious characteristic of natural building materials like wood and stone is that contrasting areas of material differ along several dimensions, not just one. For example, a knot in a plank of wood contrasts with the surrounding straight grain in terms of shape and color, as well as in density and strength. In general, the dimensions of contrast in organic forms — color, size, shape, strength and granularity, for example — are functionally linked to each other, so change in any one dimension is accompanied by corresponding changes in all the others.

Therefore, if one is trying to develop an organic, natural building design, it makes sense to imitate this aspect of organic form. As you create a contrasting element — say a small alcove within a large room — you will instinctively imbue it with other contrasting qualities beyond just a smaller floor area: Give it a lower ceiling and its own spot of increased lighting, and color its walls somewhat differently to contrast with the larger room.

Parts of the environment that embody several different dimensions of contrast will, as a result, have more impact. Parts of buildings that do not follow suit can appear strange, unsatisfying or somehow wrong. An example will illustrate this point: We studied a fireplace, trying to figure out why it seemed so dull and boring. The walls of the room were covered with smooth, dark redwood boards. The fireplace was constructed of smooth, dark red bricks. Though the building elements and materials contrasted, their colors were nearly identical. They just didn't look different enough. The design solution

The smooth, dark redwood walls and mantle contrast with the rough, light stucco of the fireplace's masonry. Color contrast is achieved by adding a small amount of green tint to the white stucco.

involved changing the grain, texture and color of the fireplace with a hand-troweled coat of cement stucco, to contrast the dark, smooth redwood boards with a larger-scaled surface of light-colored, rough-textured stucco. Further, we tinted the white base color of the stucco with a little green, to contrast more strongly with the redwood, and then with a little tan, to link it back to the redwood. The result of these changes is paradoxical — the room is enlivened by the lighter color and roughened texture of the fireplace, yet it also seems a more peaceful and settled place.

Design is also influenced by the way in which construction materials are used. It is more straightforward and much easier to develop the qualities of the design from the qualities of the construction materials. When the form of the whole corresponds to the form of the parts, the construction will appear natural, or organic. For example, if a fireplace is to be built of natural stone, the design of the finished fireplace should have some of the same roundness, massiveness, darkness and unevenness of the stones. If it does not, it may appear strained, mannered or unnatural. Similarly, the application of stone veneer over plywood invariably appears artificial because a wall of genuine stacked stone could never be so vertically planar — common

sense insists that a stone wall be thicker at the base. Awkwardness also results from the stamping of a geometrically regular pattern into a homogeneous, continuous material such as linoleum, plastic veneer or freshly poured concrete, because the properties of the design do not correspond to the properties of the materials. Forcing materials into a form that does not emerge naturally, like trying to make tightly curved garden paths with square pavers, or false rustication (distressing wood, or painting bricks to make them look old), all lead to a sense of artificiality.

House and Function

The functional requirements that a building must satisfy — structural, thermal and spatial — produce specific recurring clusters of characteristics. Empathizing with the structural forces within the building, for example, helps to create the appropriate group of contrasts between the foundation and the walls and between the walls and the roof structure.

In his book, *What It Feels Like to Be a Building* (Washington, D. C.: Preservation Press, 1988), Forrest Wilson teaches structure by analogy, presenting groups of qualities that make both structural and intuitive sense. For example, he pictures the stones at the base of a cathedral wall as being short, wide and heavy men, in contrast to the taller, thinner and lighter figures at the top of the wall. Similarly, the flying buttresses are stout, compacted rams, in contrast to the roof rafter ties, which are thin, elongated men.

Just as materials can be deceptive — with Formica looking like granite and wallboard looking like continuous plaster — so can the structure of a building be opaque to our understanding. With enough metal connectors and hold-downs, the structural engineer can make almost any house buildable, no matter how structurally insensitive the design. But it is also possible to design buildings that look solid, houses that visually explain how they gain their strength to stand.

Contrast theory demands that the bases of walls contrast somehow with the tops of walls. Structural empathy and understanding suggest that a way to do that is to make the bases wider and thicker, heavier and harder, composed of bulkier, large-scale elements that are darker, rougher and colder. By contrast, the tops of walls will be lighter and more delicate, composed of small-scale details and elements.

In this empathetic representation of a cathedral's structure, we can see that short, wide and heavy belong together, as do tall, thin and light. (Drawing by Forrest Wilson.)

The thermal requirements for a building can also produce tightly integrated groups of qualities, specifying, for example, how the north side of a building should be contrasted with the south. We show some thermally influenced designs later in the book, but here we'll point out that a typical passive-solar house is dug into a south-facing slope, minimizing its northern exposure and opening up its windows to the south to capture winter sunlight. The result is a cool north facade, which is dark, low and empty. It contrasts strongly with the warm south facade, which is light, high and full. The particular form the contrasts take is primarily a response to the thermal design of the building in relation to the sun.

Beyond structural and thermal functioning lies the much larger, more complex area of the inhabitants' functional needs. A substantial part of a house's design grows out of a response to users' common needs. Thus functional spaces will often have a cluster of common qualities. A workroom or laundry will be hard, cool, light and large in contrast to a soft, warm, dark, small fireplace alcove. Each group of attributes arises from the different functional needs of each area.

House and Culture

The links between the dimensions of contrast are embodied in the history of building. They exist in our cultural memory and in our language. As we recall those houses that are particulary memorable, themes emerge as clusters of contrasts. We begin to recognize the archetypal power of:

a foundation that is short, thick, heavy and hard;

a shady, cool, low, blank, north side;

a tall, sunny, warm, moist greenhouse;

a dim, warm, ordered library, full of rich detail.

Conversely, when a place is designed with disregard for these interrelationships, its qualities will probably not cohere to form a unified impression. Disjointed or jarring qualities may result. Thus, the dimensions of contrast within some part of a building can either cooperate and reinforce each other, or they can fight each other.

On the facing page is a sketch of semantic congruency for the dimensions of contrast, summarizing how words are typically paired. Although this isn't visible in the sketch, some of the pairs are strongly linked, like dark/in and up/out. Other associations are weak, such as down/mystery and in/full. The remaining pairs are moderately linked. But taken together, the six interconnected dimensions constitute a system. The linked dimensions are like facets of a single entity.

The Good House

We end this theoretical part of the book by inviting you to recall from your experience a specific house, one you found powerful or beautiful. Picture it now in your mind's eye. Regardless of whether it is large or small, expensive or modest, tall or low, aged or contemporary, it can probably be described as follows:

From a distance, even as you squint to see it, it can be recognized as an entity, a specific thing. It is not just part of the environment; rather, it has a presence, like a recognized face in a crowd.

It is composed of different parts, which have joined to form the whole. You can see both the parts and the whole at the same time. It is satisfying to sort out the pieces, to disassemble the parts visually and then to reassemble them.

The parts of the house are not identical to each other. Some are higher, farther out or darker than others — the parts contrast.

But even so, the contrasting parts are connected and linked. If one part is light and its neighbor is dark, they are linked by a third mediating part, or joint.

Each instance of a quality is accompanied by its opposite. Wherever there is highness, it will be joined by some degree of lowness. Even a simple area will contain at least some trace of complexity.

The house contains every possible kind of contrast. It has something to say about exposed and tempered, up and down, in and out, and so on, through all six dimensions.

These statements about the parts and their relationships apply to all levels of scale throughout the house — from the site plan through the internal arrangement of spaces, down to the details of construction and material.

Finally, the contrasts embodied in each part of the good house tend to agree and reinforce each other. The result is poetic, resonating with many overtones of harmony.

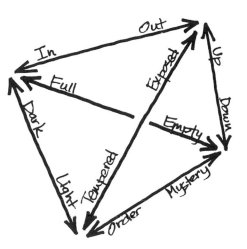

The six interrelated dimensions of contrast. The poles of each dimension are associated with each other.

SECTION 2:
PRACTICE

9

FOUR HOUSES MADE OF CONTRAST

In the first section of the book, we presented a theory of contrast and examined the basic types of contrast that occur in works of architecture. We isolated each type and explained it with examples. But the dimensions of contrast don't exist independently, and ultimately, to form a building, designers are faced with the task of working with all the dimensions simultaneously. It is therefore time to turn our attention away from the parts—the dimensions of contrast—and to begin to look at the whole—buildings made from strong contrasting elements.

In this chapter, we'll look at how four different buildings embody our ideas; we'll explore the ways in which the designers, working under different conditions, simplify, elaborate and overlay the dimensions of contrast as they struggle to bring them together in balanced composition. We have chosen the examples to cover a range of climates, styles and complexities of program to underscore the fact that our ideas are not inherently linked to a certain architectural, regional or cultural building style. We have also chosen these projects because, quite simply, they are fascinating buildings from which there is much to learn. They are arranged in ascending order of complexity, like a set of lessons.

First, there is a modernist courtyard house in the woods of Connecticut, a simple primer of sharp contrasts. Second is another courtyard house, but this one is in a desert climate and draws deeply on vernacular traditions. The third structure is a Craftsman-style house in northern California, whose strength lies in the subtlety of its weave of formal and informal order. The fourth example is another California house (in our opinion, a real masterpiece), which combines all the dimensions of contrast in a singular harmonious composition.

The Noyes House

New Canaan, Connecticut designed by Eliot Noyes (1955)

This house is dramatically, and deceptively, simple — a patio home in the Connecticut woods. The massive stone wall that surrounds it, broken only by a central wide gate, suggests that visitors are arriving at a place set starkly apart from the woods. But if we were to approach this stone wall, open the gate and step in, we would find that we were not quite in. We would certainly be inside the great wall and under the cover of a breezeway, but we would be on the edge of a large, rather formal patio and in the midst of a variety of contrasts.

The most obvious contrast is the one embodied by the patio itself, for although it is within the enclosure, it is also an outside space, open to the sky and to the treeline. The private, enclosed, crisply defined patio also contrasts sharply with the woods beyond, which are public, open, undefined and natural. The walls on either side of the patio offer additional contrast — one is glass, the other wood siding. Behind the glass is the wing that houses the common spaces (kitchen and dining/living room); the private spaces (bedrooms, bathrooms and storage) are behind the wood wall.

The house that architect Eliot Noyes designed for himself in 1955 is a stark essay in the most elementary dimensions of contrast: in/out and solid/void. (Photos by Ezra Stoller, © Esto.)

Across the patio from the entry gate, a second stone wall mirrors the entry wall. (This wall also has a gate at its center, leading to the woods.) This and the first stone wall contain and protect the two transparent walls of glass at each end of the house; the strength of the house lies in this interplay between the heavy, opaque stone and the light, transparent glass. Turning in a circle, we alternately experience the permanent, unchanging stone and, through the glass, the ever-changing play of light on trees. The stone conceals, the glass reveals.

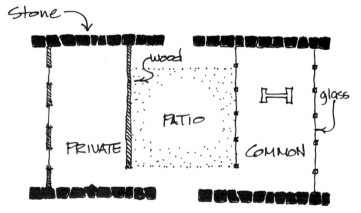

Because the patio is at the geometric center of the house, it becomes, paradoxically, the most interior of the building's spaces.

The fireplace wall at the center of the living room echoes, in miniature, the overall theme of the house — heavy stone walls clasping a light, contrasting element.

Wall of books

Stone walls

Plaster wall above

This bedroom is a modernist cave—a solid stone back with a delicate glass front. (Photo by Ezra Stoller, © Esto.)

The fireplace near the center of the commons separates the living area from a library/study. Its construction echoes that of the house itself, at a smaller scale. Two stone walls flank and contain a contrasting element between them. On the fireplace side, this element is a smooth plaster wall; on the library side, it is a wall of books.

In the private wing, the bedrooms are also made of a mix of solid and glass walls. But here solid walls predominate. Each bedroom is like a cave, with a solid corner/back looking out a glass front to the woods beyond. It is interesting to note how the architect shifts the balance of stone and glass through the house, from commons to private rooms. In the commons, glass dominates, and the feeling of the space is open and expansive, anchored by the stone. In the sleeping rooms, the solid walls dominate, creating a secure resting place from which one may look out to the openness beyond.

Another sharp contrast is drawn between exposure to and protection from the elements (see pp. 21-28). You can see in the drawing at right that there are, in effect, two houses, one private and one public. In inclement weather, residents crossing from one to the other can walk along the edge of the patio, where they will be sheltered but still exposed to the outdoor temperature. Knowing that a toasty room is but a few steps away encourages enjoyment of even the worst the weather has to offer. In this way, the house dramatically frames the experience of a crisp, snowy night with the warmth of a heated place.

Although this house presents some clear, strong contrasts, it does not possess all of the dimensions discussed in the first section of this book. For example, it does not offer contrasts between up and down or light and dark. It does not explore the contrasts of flat roof and gable roof, machinecraft and handcraft, geometric order and mystery. Nor does the house link the contrasts that it does explore in subtle ways, for example, by joining the stone walls to the glass walls with intermediary elements.

The Noyes house is spare and elegant in the best modernist sense. But while it gains power and focus

The edge of the patio shields occupants from the elements as they cross from one wing to another.

from its bold, even stark, manipulation of a few contrasting elements, for people whose images of home are not fully captured by modernist precepts, the house seems austere, flat, too much the machine for living. In the terms of this book, we can say that the house suffers from too lean a diet of contrast; it is not richly enough dimensioned with contrasting themes. Working from its limited palette, it is a beautifully crafted work of art, but it may be that most people simply do not wish to live in a work of art, at least not in the limited 20th-century Western sense of art. Perhaps the places we wish to call home require a richer blend of old and new, high and low, clean and frilly than this house, ultimately, is able to convey.

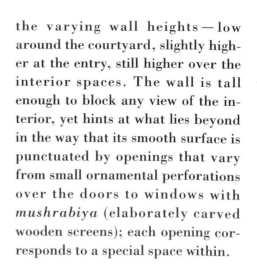

The Hamdy House

Cairo, Egypt
designed by Abdel Wahed El-Wakil
(1978)

Though it is simple and small (only 1,115 sq. ft.), this courtyard house offers a rich array of contrasts. The form and details reflect the local climate and culture, but the building as a whole has a universal appeal, which is derived from the spatial, thermal, textural and visual contrasts it expresses.

In plan, the house is rectangular, a simple white solid punctured by windows and doors of various scales. As you approach the entry, the richness within is suggested by the varying wall heights — low around the courtyard, slightly higher at the entry, still higher over the interior spaces. The wall is tall enough to block any view of the interior, yet hints at what lies beyond in the way that its smooth surface is punctuated by openings that vary from small ornamental perforations over the doors to windows with *mushrabiya* (elaborately carved wooden screens); each opening corresponds to a special space within.

The entry is a study in contrasts. A deep arch in an otherwise flat, rectangular wall, it is the only possible way into the compound, which clearly is designed to keep passersby out. Under the arch it is cool and shady, in contrast to the bright surroundings. As pedestrians pass through the outer door into this small, low-ceilinged alcove, they are still literally outdoors but very much inside the complex. As in the Noyes house, an open courtyard lies ahead, a protected version of out. The process of moving from out through in to out, light to dark to light, creates a rhythm of entry, a series of linked contrasts that precedes the approach to the main door — a final threshold crossed upon arrival.

On the scale of the whole building, the house and courtyard can be viewed as a situation where in stands alone in a field of out (see p. 15), yet once you have moved

The simple rectangular form of the Hamdy house encloses a courtyard and home of great complexity. (Photo by Abdel Wahed El-Wakil.)

through the entry, the theme is reversed: Out (the courtyard) is cradled by in (the walls surrounding the building). The entry alcove links the two, combining elements of both, enclosed yet open.

The courtyard carries the link between in and out still further, balancing spaces that are exterior and exposed to the elements with those that are comparatively tempered. One edge contains a deep seating alcove under an arched roof with windows to the exterior (see the photo at right). It provides a shady, dry spot from which to observe the courtyard. A few steps down to the center of the court and it is bright, wet (from the fountain) and exposed. Either space on its own could be wonderful; the chance to experience both simultaneously makes this area special. The fountain, which is at the lowest point, brings life to the courtyard. It links low and high, water and air, providing a permanent boundary and the mystery of ever-changing reflections.

Inside, the smallness of the house becomes obvious, consisting as it does of only a living area, dining room, kitchen and sleeping loft. To create variety, the designer manipulated the size and shapes of the spaces, the degree to which each space is separated from an adjacent space and the thickness of the surrounding walls.

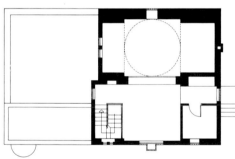

The entry courtyard is an open space, yet it has all the complexity and form of a room. The surrounding walls create a sense of security and permanence. (Photo by Abdel Wahed El-Wakil.)

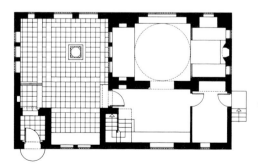

Designing a space of so few rooms to provide expression of a full range of feelings is a challenge. Here the designer used different room shapes and sizes to create variety. (Drawing by Abdel Wahed El-Wakil.)

83

The warm colors, the heat from the fire and the soft form of the fireplace contrast with the ordered geometry of the cool-white living area to create an intimate retreat. (Photo by Abdel Wahed El-Wakil.)

Of all the rooms, the living area is the largest. Covered by a high domed ceiling, it is formally and symmetrically organized, an imposing room of grand proportions. This volume might be intimidating if it were not contrasted by the scale of the fireplace alcove, where soft carpets and cushions on raised ledges invite residents to sit in an area sized for intimate conversation. An occupant's experience in this room encompasses large and small, hard and soft, casual and formal — you can sit by the fire in a protected space or stand exposed beneath the skylights in the open dome high above. These extremes are related by proximity as well as by a geometry that includes both the linear and rectangular forms of a rational order and the domical or rounded surfaces of a more natural order. The space feels rational because of the choice of a cube as the primary form in the hierarchy. The scale of subsidiary spaces gradually diminishes from the high center through lower alcoves into smaller window niches, and in the application of symmetries and subsymmetries in the organization of space. Yet this almost mathematical order is inextricably linked with forms that recall nature. The dome, perforated by small skylights, recalls a starry skydome; the bulge of the fireplace suggests a fire at the mouth of a cave. Occupants thus feel part of both worlds.

The living area gains a sense of importance from its thick walls. Windows are set in reveals that are deep enough to feel like display shelves or seats; existing in the space between in and out, they link this room to the outside while demonstrating just how protected it really is. The window details extend this sense of protection. While the surround is simple white plaster, the window frame itself is made of dark, ornately carved wood, a filigree that admits and filters light yet simultaneously establishes a strong barrier to the outside (see the photo on the facing page).

The up/down dimension of this building is most powerfully felt in the link between the living and dining areas. The high living-room ceiling creates a light, airy feel, like a bower lit by tiny skylights. It is in sharp contrast to the dark, low-ceilinged entry and dining areas. The narrow, dark, winding staircase at the end of the entry hints at the upstairs sleeping loft; the heavy exposed beams clearly support a load above. The balcony in the loft overlooks the living area, interconnecting up and down by allowing the opportunity to experience both at once, in the same way that the seating alcove in the courtyard encourages the enjoyment of contrasting experiences (see the building section on the facing page).

Unlike the previous house, where all the contrasts were bold and striking, many of the contrasts in this house are experienced on a subtle, even subliminal, level. The floor of the living area, for example, steps up at one end to the warmth and light of the fireplace, recalling the contrasting experience of stepping down in the courtyard to the coolness of water. In both spaces, there are simple plaster sitting ledges built out from the walls — the house invites its users to stop and enjoy the fire or water. At the entries, subtle clues speak about the quality of the space to be entered: The door from the outside of the building to the courtyard is recessed (out penetrates in), while the front door of the house sits under a projected portion of the wall above (in penetrates out).

This sense of interrelating experiences is the real strength of El-Wakil's design. Where warmth is experienced, coolness is recalled; entering indoor spaces recalls the contrast when entering outdoor spaces. The fundamental order of this house establishes changes of level, passages from light to dark, transitions from enclosed to open, areas of dense opacity and light filigree, always reminding us of the opposing condition.

With its low ceiling and dark wood beams, the dining area feels almost cave-like beside the openness of the living area. (Photo by Abdel Wahed El-Wakil.)

The building section reveals the strong similarity between the forms and development of the interior and the courtyard. (Drawing by Abdel Wahed El-Wakil.)

The Schneider House

Berkeley, California
designed by Bernard Maybeck
(1907)

The overall shape, the floor-plan and the detailing of this house all offer rich lessons in how linked contrasts can be used to create an exciting design. Although we don't have a record of what Maybeck was thinking during the design of this building, we'll look at some ideas that might have entered into his thought process, beginning with the largest-scale concepts and ending with several details.

The house is built toward the top of a hill, on a sloped lot with a superb view of San Francisco Bay to the west. Approaching the entry from the street below, you pass through an impressive garden (originally planned by John McLaren, creator of Golden Gate Park), whose softly rounded forms contrast with the strong, linear geometry of the house. The house, shown in the photo on p. 88, is a two-story cube-like volume covered with a gable roof whose ridge runs north/south; the tall south-facing gable end of the building gives generous light to the children's rooms upstairs and the dining and living rooms downstairs (see the south elevation). But because the view is to the west, the house also has a contrasting inter-

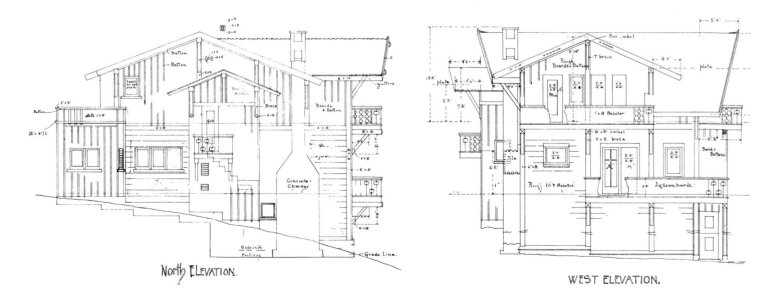

NORTH ELEVATION.

WEST ELEVATION.

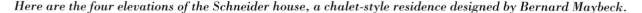

Here are the four elevations of the Schneider house, a chalet-style residence designed by Bernard Maybeck.

secting roof with an east/west ridge, defining the west-facing view of the upstairs master bedroom and the west end of the downstairs living room (see the west elevation). These roofs are linked with 6-ft. wide overhangs, which overlap and interlock.

Another large-scale contrast embodied in the house is that between up and down. Orienting the untreated redwood siding horizontally on the lower floor and vertically on the upper floor divided the house into two distinct parts. Up is then linked to down with attached volumes, which cling to each facade of the primary cube. The south facade has an entryway topped with a deck serving the children's bedrooms above; the north facade has a stairway pro-

truding from the main volume at the landing, covered by its own north/south ridged roof; the east facade has a utility room topped with a deck serving the upstairs bath; and the west facade has a second-floor deck off the master bedroom.

These smaller, secondary volumes carry the vertical siding of the upper floor back down to the ground (see particularly the north elevation), and create a contrast between large and small. Since each appendage is differently dimensioned and roofed, all the small volumes contrast with one another. But they are also linked by the uniform vertical siding and by the fact that their roof or deck railing is below the overall main roof.

SOUTH ELEVATION

EAST ELEVATION

A view of the Schneider house from the southwest corner shows its use of several interconnected contrasts: big and small, horizontal and vertical, plain and fancy. (Photo by Robert Bernhardi.)

A final large-scale gesture worth noting is the way in which the contrasting south and west facades are linked with an elegant porch, which begins on the south as the entry stairs, temporarily becomes enclosed to form the entry and then breaks through and continues along the south facade, turning the corner and wrapping almost the entire living room. The porch links the south and west facades together into a unified composition, as shown in the photo at left. This photo illustrates how each element of the building is independently developed to gain strength, vigor and identity, then linked into a harmonious whole with the interwoven roofs, the brackets that pull the wildly projecting overhangs and balconies into the main volume and the unifying corner balcony wrapping around the living room.

Now that we have looked at the building as an overall volume from the outside, let's look inside at the plan. In one sense, it's a conventional three-bedroom, one-and-one-half-bath plan, with all of the common areas downstairs and all the private ones upstairs. It's deceptively simple, consisting, as we have said, of a central cube surrounded with attached spaces, which are arranged informally according to function. But downstairs, Maybeck created magic out of a 14-ft. by 24-ft. living room, a 14-ft. by 14-ft.

dining room and some artfully arranged circulation space. He achieved this by linking all the elements together with formal symmetries and subsymmetries.

Here is a hypothetical sequence of design decisions that might have generated the floor plan of the downstairs rooms. Maybeck started by dividing the available square footage of public space into two distinct, contrasting parts — the large living space and the smaller dining area. These are linked together with wide pocket doors in between; the doorway is emphasized by being positioned at the center of an axis that runs through the approximate centers of the two rooms (axis 1 in the floor plan). The windows at each end of the axis (a main living-room window on the west and a main dining-room window on the east) further reinforce the linking power of the doorway and its axis.

The two main spaces are additionally bound to each other by the circulation space between them. This space runs north and south, establishing a new axis B, which is perpendicular to axis 1. Maybeck did not relegate the circulation space to a hallway — instead, he welded it to the living room by treating it as an arcade along one edge of the larger room, separated only by freestanding 10-in. square wooden box posts. These elements define the relation-

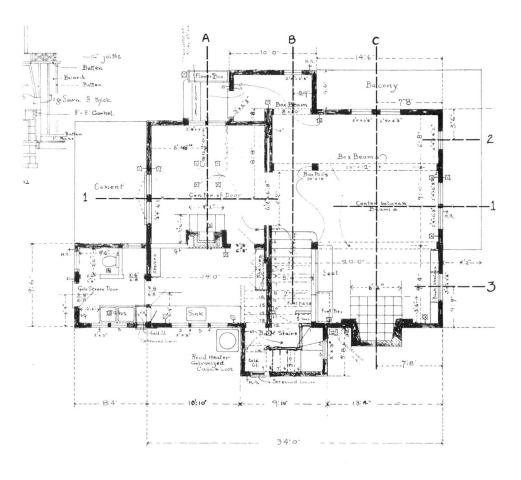

The plan of the house is a simple rectangular box, with subsidiary volumes attached to each of the four sides as needed. The common rooms downstairs are developed around a series of major and minor axes, which allows the spaces to be both distinct individuals and parts of a flowing, interconnected whole.

The oversized fireplace has built-in seating and a storage cabinet that replaces a conventional mantel.

fireplace contrasts the warm inside part of the room with the cool outside window wall. (Because axis A runs through the center of the outdoor porch, it also links the porch to the dining room.)

The circulation space is developed with its own axis (axis B), which is defined by a new window in the foyer at the south end, and by the stairs that ascend to the upper floor at the other end.

The living room centers on axis C, defined with a window at one end and a major fireplace at the other end. These elements are linked and balanced in terms of temperature, because the fire is placed on the cool, northern side and the windows on the warmer, southern side. Finally, the living room is broken down into three contrasting subsections, which reinforce the north/south distinction. The box posts, overhead ceiling beams and major west window are all centered on axis 1, and they define the center, or heart, of the living room. And by defining a middle, two surrounding subspaces are defined. The southern part of the living room is the sunniest, most active space, since it is closest to the entry and can overlook the entry garden and path by a balcony. The northern part is quietest and most sheltered. With its massive fireplace and built-in seating (doubling as a wood-storage

ships between the dining, living and circulation spaces. Each space in turn is embellished and then developed by subsidiary elements.

The centeredness and presence of the dining room is increased by a new perpendicular axis of symmetry (axis A), anchored by a large window at its south end and a dining-room fireplace at its north end. The

box), it is the heart of the house, solid and dark, with only a single small window, which was originally embedded into a built-in bookshelf.

One result of all these plan decisions is that the downstairs feels spacious and open, even though it is composed of cozy, well-proportioned subspaces—it feels big and small at the same time. The fireplace inglenook, for example, is only 10 ft. by 15 ft., but from it you can look along an uninterrupted diagonal length of over 40 ft. to the corner of the dining room. And the entire suite of common spaces has a center of balance—at the intersection of axis 1 and axis B on the floor plan—which gives the downstairs a restful, settled feeling.

The upstairs plan has two interesting features. The two spaces that are fitted with plumbing—the bath and kitchen—are stacked in the shady northeast corner; both bath and kitchen are treated as mechanical service spaces, leaving the sunnier orientations for the living rooms. And the stairway down from the bedrooms has a portion called "servants' stairs," which breaks off from the main stairway at the landing and heads down to the kitchen rather than to the living room, reinforcing the distinction between served and service spaces. The bedrooms, on the other hand, are clearly rooms that are meant to be

lived in. They are graced with walk-in closets and double 2-ft. 6-in. by 6-ft. 8-in. "windows," which allow access to decks protected by the generous roof overhangs.

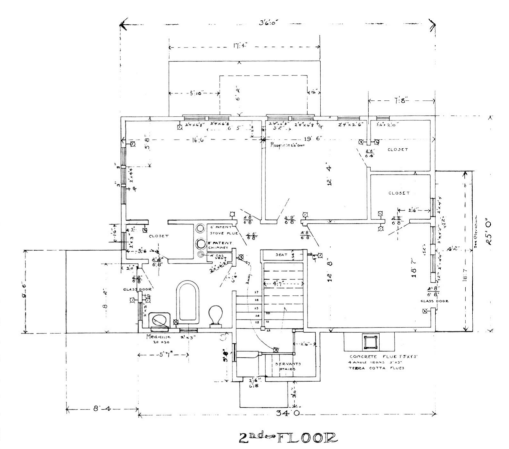

2nd FLOOR

SCALE ¼ INCH · 1 FOOT

Upstairs, the service spaces—kitchen, bath and stairs—are placed on the shady north, enabling the living spaces—bedrooms—to have sunny south and west orientations.

*Note the
contrast between
the corner
balusters (the
apples) and the
middle balusters
(the spindles).*

Many of the details of the Schneider house are enlivened by the skillful use of linked contrasts. Careful examination of the original elevations shows that Maybeck intended the deck balusters at the corner to contrast with those in the middle. In the actual construction, this contrast was executed very beautifully. The corner boards were scroll-cut to form apples from the voids; the center boards, however, were cut so that the boards themselves formed the figure of the pattern — a spindle shape. You can see the effect of this contrast in the photo above.

Looking again at the living-room fireplace inglenook (see the photo on p. 90), notice the vigorous contrast between the small-scale roughness of the brickwork in the fireplace and the broad smoothness of the wide redwood boards everywhere else. The link between them is the ever-present dark, warm, reddish color that they both share. (A criticism often leveled at Maybeck's houses, however, is that there is insufficient color contrast, that the overuse of dark, warm color leads some to feel a kind of "redwood indigestion.") On the building's exterior, the relative smoothness of the walls contrasts with the rougher texture of the carved deck balusters.

Another contrast to note is that between plain and fancy. All the exterior elements of the building — siding boards, trim, door and window sash — are of unpainted, unstained redwood. The fancy-cut deck balusters are perhaps one attempt to temper this austerity. Another clear and humorous play on the contrast between plain and fancy appears in one window on the south facade, which is fancifully trimmed out, perhaps to announce it is part of the entry foyer (refer to the south elevation on p. 87).

The relentless straight lines of the building's honest, simple and exposed construction are contrasted by the dining-room fireplace with its sloping breast and fancifully sawn mantelpiece.

The plain/fancy contrast also exists in the dining room, where the straight lines of the interior wood panels and battens are replaced with a decoratively cut-out mantelpiece over the fireplace, a whimsical and relaxed foil to the overall rigor of the design and construction of the house.

This house can be viewed as an essay on the contrast between the discipline of formal order (including interlocked axes of symmetry and simple construction) on the one hand, and the freedom of informal planning (including contrasting facades and freely carved decorative elements) on the other. Maybeck's ability to link formality to informality makes the building exciting.

93

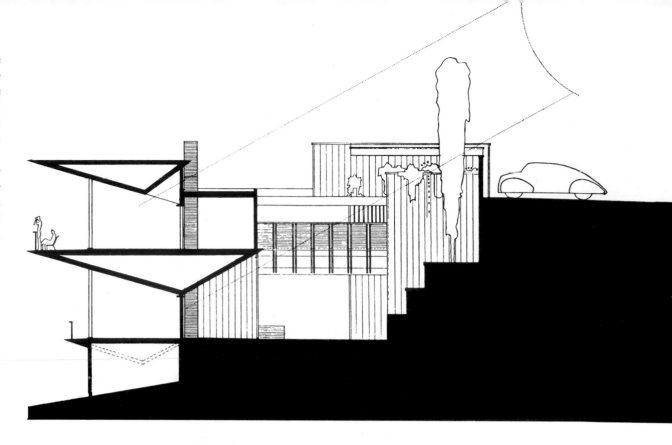

In the Havens house, the service spaces are separated from and contrasted with the living spaces. Then they are linked by the space between and by a covered bridge.

The Havens House

*Berkeley, California
designed by Harwell Hamilton
Harris (1939)*

The Havens house is in an architecturally rich neighborhood on a lot that slopes down to a magnificent view of San Francisco's Bay Area. It is often said that the character of a building is determined by the site plan, and here Harris began with a bold contrast, separating the house into two distinct parts according to function. The service spaces (garage, maid's quarters) are located up against the street, and the more private living spaces are down the hill, toward the view; the contrasting halves are then linked by a central outdoor space through which crosses a covered pedestrian bridge.

This single linked contrast is one of the keys to understanding the rest of the building. But the design isn't so simple that it can be grasped at first glance. Rather, the order of the building gradually unfolds, becoming evident as one moves through the building from the public street to the most private spaces. The building has order, but it also has mystery.

The Havens house presents high blank walls to the public, protecting a gradually unfolding private world beyond. (Photo by Roger Sturtevant.)

Look at the house from street level (see the photo above). The garage door and a 7-ft. high fence running the width of the lot block any view of the rest of the building. The only hint of an entrance is the fact that the garage door is recessed 6 ft., creating a covered place in which to search for an opening. Part of the fence pivots inward to serve as a gate. This gate leads to the top of some exterior stairs, which lead down to the bridge, though it's not immediately apparent that the structure is in fact a bridge. This in turn leads to the front door of the house.

The entrance gate leads down a flight of steps, across a covered bridge, to the front door. (Photo by Roger Sturtevant.)

95

The passageway is a mysterious space indeed. The fence gate is so solid and tight-fitting that visitors expect to find an interior space on the other side. But instead they find themselves in a passage that feels half inside and half outside — it is about half enclosed with walls, planters and openable glass, and a solid roof above. The sense of mystery is furthered by postponing views of the main ordering elements. The visitor can look up diagonally to the sky and can see the front door ahead, but the Bay Area view is entirely blocked by the building beyond, and the great central space below is blocked by the deep plant shelves and angled wooden louvers. All visitors initially know is that they are leaving the street environment and crossing through a sunny, airy transitional space toward another front door.

The entry bridge to the house is half inside, half outside.

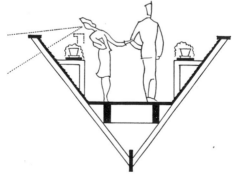

From the bridge, the view of the central open space below is blocked by plant shelves and wooden louvers.

The front door opens into a low, relatively dark, flat-ceilinged foyer dominated by a semicircular staircase descending to the left and a large coat closet directly ahead. As visitors proceed forward from the foyer, they begin to catch glimpses of the main living spaces ahead, as expected. But in contrast to the low, dark foyer, the living room is breathtakingly spacious and bright — filled with light from a continuous band of floor-to-ceiling windows along the entire south, west and north facades, allowing almost

96

overwhelming views of the Bay Area below and beyond. The flat ceiling of the foyer also gives way to a ceiling that slopes up and out, intensifying the feeling of being catapulted into the sky and view (see the photos on p. 98).

To understand this transition, look at the floor plan (see the drawings at right). The architect has again created a contrast between service and served spaces, repeating the primary site-planning theme at a secondary level of detail. The kitchen, entry foyer, stairway, guest bath and guest bedroom are grouped into a single 12-ft. wide service zone along the east side of the building; all have low, flat ceilings. In contrast, the dining room and living room comprise a 15-ft. wide served zone along the west (view) side of the building; these have a unified ceiling sloping upward from 7 ft. at the center to 15 ft. at the edge of the exterior balcony (see the building section on p. 94).

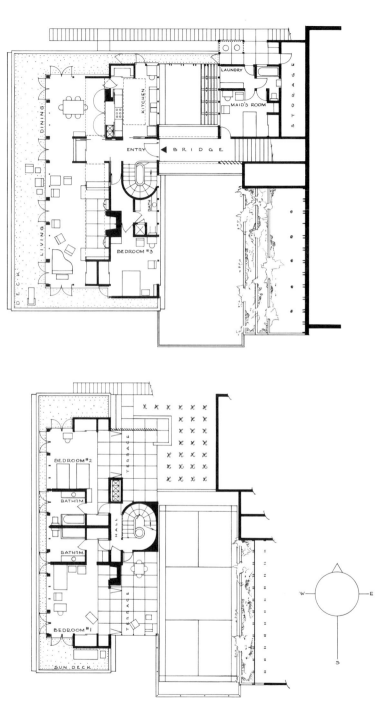

The ordered, rational floor plan is orchestrated to create surprise and wonder for the visitor. The upper entry level is shown at top left; the lower bedroom level is shown below.

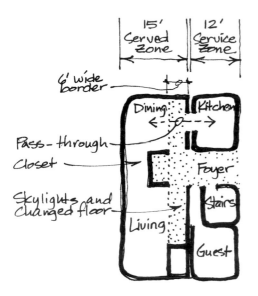

The service zone is contrasted with the served zone. The zones are then linked with closets, skylights and unique floor materials.

These two highly contrasting halves are then linked. The foyer is welded to the living space by a bold projection of closet and bookshelf into the dining/living space. The spaces are interlocked by this closet/bookshelf element. The kitchen is linked to the dining room by a pass-through counter and sideboard. A more subtle link is the 6-ft. long continuous border strip between the serving and served areas, which is defined by a change in ceiling material, a change in floor material at the hearth, a solid wall at the north, and solid closets at the south (see the drawing at left and the photo below left).

The indoors/outdoors contrast of the entry bridge is continued in these main living spaces. In contrast to the indoor feeling of the service spaces (small, low and dark), the dining and living rooms feel extraordinarily outdoors. Most of the glass in the dining and living areas is openable, and the interior floor and ceiling surfaces extend uninterrupted 9 ft. beyond the glass. Combined with the height above, the view beyond and the transparent railing of chainlink fencing, the result is a feeling of being up in the sky. Harris himself said that the Havens house was "a sky house more than an earth house."

The low-ceilinged foyer is linked to the main living spaces by the entry closet and bookshelf volume. (Photo by Roger Sturtevant.)

In contrast to the low, dark foyer, the main living spaces are oriented up and out toward the view of the bay beyond. (Photo by Roger Sturtevant.)

The winding staircase leading to the bedrooms below is unusually long (a vertical distance of about 14 ft.). Made of bent plywood and lit only by a small skylight from above and a companion light at the bottom newel post, the stair contrasts with the linearity of the house's redwood boards and bright natural lighting, so users feel as though they are descending into the hold of a ship.

The lower-floor plan continues the theme of contrasting service space with served space, with the stairway and twin bath/closets gathered into one zone. But where upstairs the service zone separated the living spaces from the great central open space, on the lower level the service spaces turn 90° to separate the two bedrooms from each other. This, then, allows each bedroom to open onto the central outdoor space.

Up to this point, the central open space between the two halves of the house had been hidden from view —from the street by the 7-ft. high fence, from the entry bridge by deep planters and louvers, from the main living spaces by the service spaces and from the stairway by the solid curved walls. This central open space, around which the entire site and building are organized, can be seen and accessed only from the lower bedrooms, the most remote, private spaces. As you step into this space from the lower bed-

rooms and look up toward the street and entry bridge, you can understand the order and organization of the house, which earlier had created only a sense of mystery.

This central space, surrounded by solid walls, overhangs and retaining walls, feels carved out of the earth. Open only to the incoming southern sun, it creates a warm, calm, quiet microclimate. Occupants feel as though they are in the palm of a protecting hand. This earth place is linked to the sky place on the west by the bedrooms themselves. Each bedroom has both a wall of openable glass connecting it to this eastern courtyard and a west-facing wall of glass opening to a balcony overlooking the Bay, just like the living spaces one floor above.

There are also linked contrasts at the smaller scale of construction details, like the smooth industrial-grey cement-board ceilings, which-contrast with the textured natural redwood walls. These materials embody a contrast along several dimensions simultaneously — texture, color and associated images (industrial vs. residential). But these contrasting materials are linked to each other by conforming to an overall 3-ft. by 3-ft. planning grid, so that the joints between the panels of cement board line up with the vertical wood columns in the west glass wall.

The curved stairway, contrasting with the linearity of the rest of the house, links the upper social spaces with the lower private ones. (Photo by Man Ray.)

The great central space around which the entire building is wrapped can be seen and accessed only from the private bedrooms on the lower level. It is the secret heart of the house. (Photo by Maynard Parker.)

The cement-board ceilings conceal an ingenious radiant-heating system, which, unlike conventional heating systems, allows the occupants to experience the contrast between heat and coolness. Heated air is circulated in the deep truss space above the ceiling and is transmitted to the room below through the ceiling panels, allowing the occupants to be warmed radiantly while surrounded by cooler air.

Refer to the floor plans on p. 97 for a final subtle contrast. Note that the maid's quarters are on the main level of the house, directly opposite the kitchen; the architect has created a clear separation between the private living spaces and the work space. But they are then linked by a separate bridge, which parallels the main entrance bridge, and by generous kitchen windows, which look back toward the windows of the living quarters.

Of all our examples, the Havens house embodies most completely and fully the concept of linked contrasts. It explores all the dimensions of architectural contrast, links the contrasts to each other, and does this at all levels of scale. The resulting house has the power to enrich our experience of life.

10
SOME CASE STUDIES

In the previous chapter, we sought to illustrate the theory of contrast by examining four projects by other architects — projects that embody our concept of the good house with varying degrees of success. Although all buildings contain contrast (every building creates an inside and an outside, for example), we saw that the contrast can be flat and conflicted, or rich and harmonious. In the Noyes house (pp. 78-81), the contrast is bold and academic, a perfect diagram of contrast, but we felt that the house would be difficult to live in. At the other end of the spectrum, the Havens house (pp. 94-100) is more strongly and richly dimensioned, a livable house that yields less readily to schematic reduction.

Whether or not readers agree with our evaluations, it's evident that the theory of contrast provides a useful language for talking about our experiences with buildings — experiences that are initially intuitive and nonverbal. But can the theory of contrast help us not only to understand and evaluate buildings, but also to generate new ones? In this chapter, we address this question by presenting several of our own projects. In each case, we explain how we employed the theory of contrast in our practice, and how it helped us with real clients, real sites and real budgets.

We begin with a remodeling project, where we tried to create strong contrast in a house considered too plain by its owners. Then we present five single-family houses, each custom-designed in participation with its users, and four multi-family housing projects of various sizes and budgets. Each of these cases explores different aspects of contrast theory. In some, the contrast is sharply etched, in others it is carefully modulated. These are projects whose design strategies were hatched in practice; for us, they have the feel of things made up as we went along. In all cases, building codes had to be accommodated and builders persuaded; clients with limited dollars had to look at drawings and models and estimates of cost and finally say, "Yes, that

seems right; let's do that." And although each house is a response to unique conditions, readers will certainly see a thread of continuity connecting these projects. We are architects practicing in the San Francisco Bay Area, and our work has been deeply influenced by the history, tradition and climate of the region.

When we begin work on a project, our clients don't ask for (nor do we try to give them) buildings that are polemical statements about Contrast in Architecture. They want buildings that work — that are functional, livable, good-looking and affordable. Of course, our job is to probe what such things mean to our clients and then to embody these meanings in form. In this way, each job, no matter what its scale, is an exploration of how we humans think about and use space. Inevitably, it seems, these explorations lead in novel directions and result in designs that neither we nor our clients would have predicted. If the design process goes well, clients not only end up with what they want, but also with something they didn't expect.

Each job, therefore, sets in motion a process that has, at its center, a vital contrast between the known (the stated program) and the unknown (what comes up as we explore the program). This is where we begin. And as the design unfolds, all the dimensions of contrast in turn come into focus. Opportunities arise, strategies are selected and choices made.

The theory of contrast, it seems, is our way of talking about what in practice we are trying to do: to create buildings that draw contrasting elements into vibrant and balanced wholes.

The Hewitt House

Berkeley, California
Architects: Jacobson, Silverstein, Winslow

Remodeling often begins with a specific functional assignment, such as adding a bedroom and bath or improving the kitchen. But sometimes there are other, less tangible issues at stake. In the case of the 50-year-old Hewitt residence, the original assignment was to remodel the kitchen, add a master bathroom and create a sunny outdoor living space off the living room. But in the process of working on the preliminary designs, it became clear that the owners were unhappy with the house in ways that were not completely expressed by their functional program. They liked the neighborhood, but had never loved the house itself.

"If we make all these improvements," the Hewitts asked, "will the house as a whole really be any better?" They worried that it wouldn't be, so they decided to look for another, more appealing house, even while we were involved in the early design stages. As they looked, we began to understand more about their tastes and saw that they had a strong appreciation for finely crafted woodwork. The building they liked most (and nearly bought) was the Arts and Crafts style Schneider house, designed early in this century by Bernard Maybeck (see pp. 86-93). It was larger than they needed, but they were enthusiastic about it in a way they had never been about their own house. They described details and expressions of craftsmanship they had found very moving. We soon realized that what the Hewitts really wanted to know was whether the remodeling job could imbue their old house with a character more in line with that of the Schneider house.

We felt this was unrealistic. There was no way a relatively small amount of remodeling could superimpose a different identity on the house. And even if we did execute each piece of their program in a contemporary version of the Arts and Crafts style, we felt the new pieces would not cohere and the whole would be a mess of conflicting parts — *ungapotchkied,* as we call it in the office.

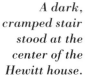

A dark, cramped stair stood at the center of the Hewitt house.

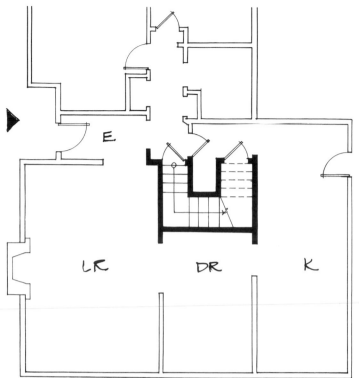

E.

LR   DR   K

As we looked through some books on Arts and Crafts houses from the turn of the century, we were impressed with the way that the staircase was often the occasion for especially beautiful design and detail. Newel posts, balusters, rails, winding treads and landings — such elements seem to bring out the best in this tradition.

In the Hewitt residence, a two-story building, the existing staircase was a cramped, narrow volume at the geometric center of the building. The staircase had originally led to the attic, but when the attic had been remodeled by previous owners into three bedrooms and a bath, this mean little space had become the central link in the traffic pattern. It began to dawn on us that even though "doing something with the staircase" was not a priority (after all, tight as it was, it got you up and down), transforming the stairs into a Craftsman centerpiece might be exactly the act that would deepen the character of the house. Remembering the disparaging remarks the Hewitts (especially Henry, who is 6 ft. 6 in. tall) had made about the stairs during one of our first visits, we began to explore the up/down dimension for ideas: the staircase as transition space...a place in its own right...an ascent to light...the landing as a stage. The Hewitts and their two teenagers are interesting, dramatic people. A

A clue for how to proceed with this project came when we realized that we were dealing with the architectural contrast between full and empty. The existing house, with its unadorned planes of plaster walls and painted trim, was, for its owners, empty; by contrast, Maybeck's building was full, nearly every inch revealing the woodworker's hands. We began to suspect that the fullness the Hewitts sought could best be created precisely within the emptiness they rejected: The empty house would be the perfect foil for a concentrated dose of craftsmanship. But how and where to do it was the question.

104

close family, they were all busy with independent lives. Perhaps the staircase could be the symbolic heart of the house, the village square of their lives.

We proposed these notions, along with a model and drawings showing a new, wider stair open to the rooms around it. Constructed of contrasting hardwoods, it would be an Arts and Crafts treasure right smack in the middle of their home and lives. The Hewitts were excited with the idea and even willing to give up parts of the functional program to achieve it within budget.

We contacted Miles Karpilow, a famed local woodworker, and within a few days he arrived at our office with full-scale mockups of staircase details. He became an active member of the design team, participating in the process from drawings through construction. It soon became clear that the stair would become the centerpiece of the house, gaining its strength through contrast with the plain white walls surrounding it. Opening up the stair to the living room, entry and dining room both enhanced the contrast between the new work and the old and linked them together. As one climbs the stair, the Craftsman styling weaves in and out of the old walls, revealing new details at each turn.

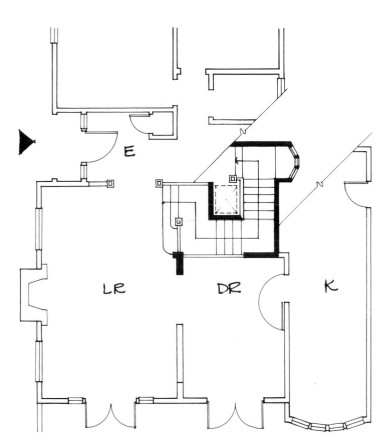

The new stair would be wider than the old one, its lower landing open like a stage to the rooms around it, and lit from above with a skylight.

In working with Karpilow, we developed the theme of contrast. To modulate the bold contrast between the stair and the house, we selected subtly contrasting woods: oak for the treads to match the existing floors, and maple for the risers. To emphasize the details of newels and balustrade, cherry was combined with maple. The cherry creates a dark, rich contrast with the white walls and will darken as it ages. The maple accents the cherry at the revealed core of the newels and the short bars between the balusters, and creates a tone that is visually

The new stair in the Hewitt house provides a symbolic center in this project — a concentrated dose of craftsmanship in the middle of the house. (Photo by John Hauf.)

The lower landing is like a stage, open to the dining room, living room, and entry. (Photo by John Hauf.)

between the cherry, the oak and the walls. Thus it acts as a binding force in the light/dark composition.

Finally, we linked the contrast between the stair and the house by adding exterior fencing and balcony rails that echo, in redwood, the central baluster pattern. This treatment at the edges of the house hints at the treatment in the center, rendering the contrast between empty (the house) and full (the stairs) more striking and less stark. Like the development of a musical theme, the richness of the center is made greater and more vibrant by introducing the motif of the center as a boundary around the empty field. The boundary defines the empty space as an entity unto itself; the area of emptiness then links the fullness at the center of the house and the fullness at the edges. This device also acts as a visual link between the inside and outside of the house.

The rest of the remodeling was completed according to the original program. The kitchen was thoroughly renovated, an upstairs bedroom was enlarged and a bathroom added, and a south-facing deck was attached to the living room—nearly every space in the house was modified. Each area was designed to extend, improve and harmonize with the older house, but contrast was subordinated to provide the stairway at the center with a strong foil.

The selection of contrasting woods —oak, maple and cherry—for the construction details modulates the overall contrast of the Craftsman stair and white walls. (Photo by Charles Miller.)

The detailing of the exterior deck rail echoes in redwood the baluster pattern of the stair. (Photo by John Hauf.)

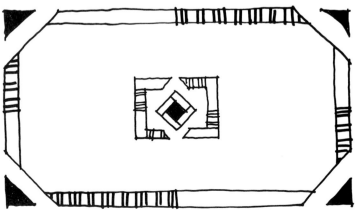

In this diagram, as in the Hewitt remodeling design, contrast is enriched by reflecting the central theme at the boundary, leavintg a positive empty space between.

107

The Osman House

Oakland, California
Architects: Jacobson, Silverstein

Our client Robbie Osman owned a house in Oakland, a bungalow crammed close to the street. The narrow yard behind the house bulged into a substantial, rectangular piece of land. Osman's unusual concept was to build a more private residence for himself in the back and to rent out the existing house.

Like most clients, Osman had a limited budget for his new house, but one of his main hopes was for a feeling of spaciousness within. Osman's bachelor status made it possible to design a small (1,570-sq. ft.) one-room house in which all the secondary spaces (entry, kitchen, study and sleeping areas) are al-coves off the two-story-high living space, gathered around a huge window. This window allows the large old willow tree to the south of the building to be appreciated from inside, and since all the secondary spaces are gathered around the window, it is visible from every room. This strategy makes the house feel much larger than it actually is.

We sited the house so as to preserve and intensify the contrast between public and private, as well as to augment the feeling of spaciousness. We placed it as far as possible on the northern side of the yard, giving breathing room to the willow tree. This allowed the building to behave as a solid, well-defined rear boundary to the long, skinny yard, as well as to hide the rectangular southern portion of the yard from casual view. The resulting south-facing garden and facade have an idyllic feeling — quiet, hidden, totally private, yet fully open to the sun and yard. Much of the house's character comes from this combination of secrecy from the city and openness to nature.

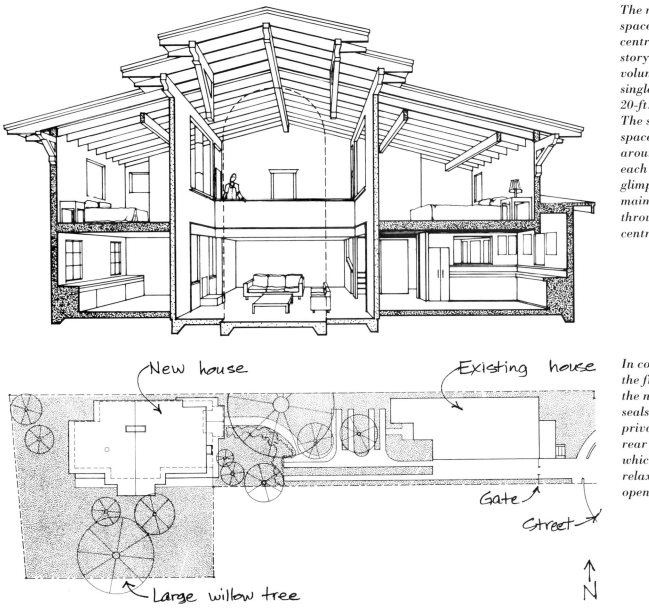

The main living space is a central two-story-high volume lit by a single 9-ft. by 20-ft. window. The secondary spaces gather around this core, each getting a glimpse of the main view through the central space.

New house

Existing house

Gate

Street

Large willow tree

N

In contrast to the front house, the new house seals off a private, quiet rear yard, into which it can relax and open itself.

Once we had a site plan, we began to develop the floor plan. We started with one large interior living space apart from and in contrast to the willow tree and its exterior space (A in the drawing below). We con- nected the two with a large, high opening — the central window. We then surrounded the living space with subsidiary spaces, roughly sym- metrical around the primary axis of living space/tree space (B). Then we connected each subsidiary space to the central space with various de- grees of openness and defined the openings with beams overhead (C).

Adding a fire/water axis (fireplace/ kitchen sink) at right angles to the living space/tree space axis in- creased the centeredness of the liv- ing space (D in the drawing on the facing page). We then created con- trast in the subsidiary spaces by differentiating their smaller parts, trying to give each of them a closed, whole shape so they would be per- ceived as entities (E). For example, we broke the eating space into two parts, contrasting the cooking area with the dining area, then recon- nected and linked them back to each other with a beamed opening.

We centered each subsidiary space with new axes of symmetry, estab- lished with windows and appliances (F), and intensified all these steps by repeating the entire procedure for the upper floor (G). Note how the upper spaces copy the relationships of the lower one: Bedrooms are open to the main living space, and an up- per walkway lies directly over the lower circulation path. This ties the floors together, creating a unity.

Design process for the Osman house: (A) Connect inside and outside with a huge central window. (B) Center the main space with surrounding smaller spaces. (C) Connect the large space to the smaller ones with beamed openings.

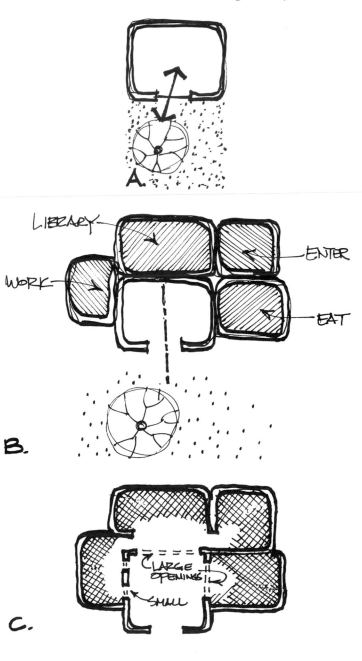

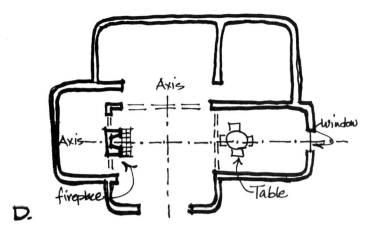

D.

(D)
Increase the centeredness of the main space.
(E)
Differentiate the parts of the smaller spaces.
(F)
Center the small spaces with new axes of symmetry.
(G)
Create a unity within the house by tying the two floors together. The upper-floor plan copies the lower-floor plan: Bedrooms are above the work area and kitchen; the upper balcony is above the circulation space.

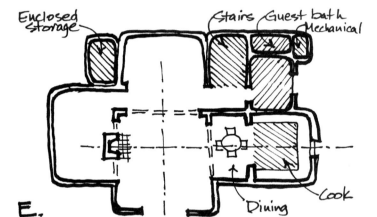

E.

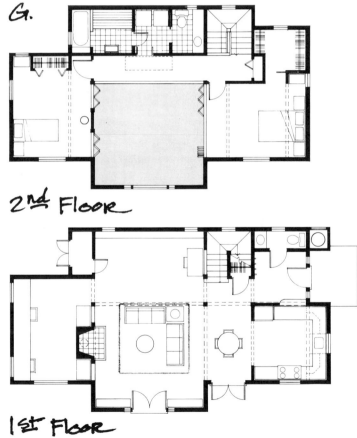

G.

2nd Floor

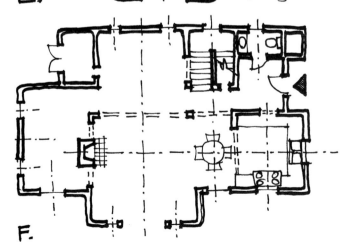

F.

1st Floor

111

The rough structural framing of the house was planned so that it could remain fully exposed, contrasting with the smooth, highly finished wallboard.

The interior construction of the house continues with the theme of contrast at the level of materials selection and finish details. Osman wanted the house to have some of the qualities of a workshop or warehouse — straightforward, economical, tough-minded, generous space. But he had a simultaneous, contrasting ethic, desiring clean, white, neutral surfaces on which to display the many beautiful artworks (including carpets, bowls and masks) he owns. To satisfy the workshop feeling, the wooden joist framing and crossbracing, as well as the metal connectors, are left exposed and unpainted. Contrasting strongly with the rough elements are the creamy,

passive surfaces of white wallboard, which makes an ideal background for Osman's collections.

These two contrasting construction elements are linked by careful detailing and neat workmanship. The exposed rafters, for example, were spaced to ensure that the last rafter at the edge of the room would project over the underlying wallboard precisely the same amount as the blocking between the rafters. This detail creates a simple, unified band of wood running around the top of the walls, which acts as trim. The exposed wood crossbracing was so carefully cut and nailed that it functions as a decorative element. With precise detailing and meticulous craftsmanship, rough structural elements can relate to more delicate and finished elements.

On the exterior, the budget dictated plywood-sheathed walls, which we left unstained but enlivened by changing the direction and spacing of plywood grooves at mid-height, contrasting the upper story with the lower. We connected these contrasting parts with a waistband of plywood and superimposed battens. In contrast to this horizontal banding between the upper and lower stories, the central double-height living space is sheathed as a single, vertical element.

This project deals mainly with the contrasts between up/down, order/mystery and in/out. From any point in the building, you are aware of your position relative to the open floor plan below and the exposed roof above. The geometry is very strong and concentrated, culminating its focus on a shaggy old backyard willow tree. Similarly, the well-behaved wallboard surfaces contrast with the rougher quality of the structural framing. Finally, the central high interior space imitates the outside with its 30-ft. height, its internal wall material of exterior redwood and its inclusion of the willow tree as its "fourth wall."

The building deals mainly with contrasts between high and low, in and out, and differing levels of finish. It is both a rough warehouse in the city and a refined temple in the woods.

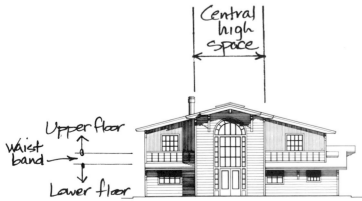

On the facade, the upper and lower floors are distinguished by different exterior plywood patterns and linked by an intermediate waistband of a third pattern. The central high space is sheathed with a continuous pattern from top to bottom.

113

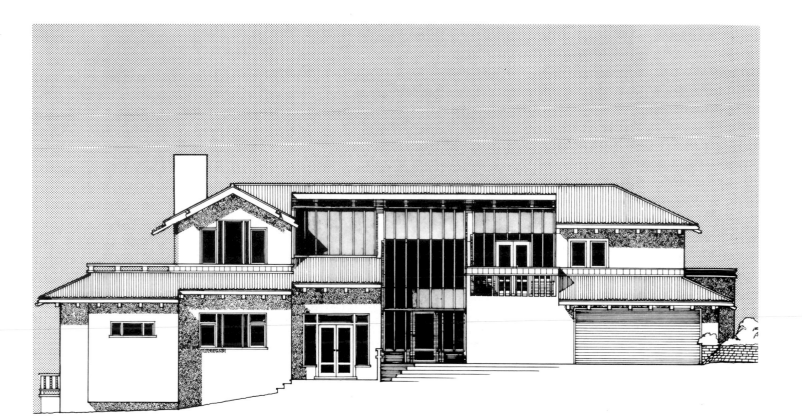

The Penn house links a traditional residential feeling with the contrasting industrial materials of corrugated roofing and large areas of metal-framed glass.

The Penn House

Berkeley, California
Architects: Jacobson, Silverstein

In our initial discussions with Jon and Carol Penn, we immediately saw that one of our primary tasks would be to reconcile their contradictory images of the new house. On the one hand, the Penns spoke of it as being substantially residential, with an air of tradition and formality, permanence and solidity: They hoped the house would be at home among its elegant old Berkeley neighbors. On the other hand, they described a somewhat industrial look of light, clean lines, large sheets of glass and white walls minimally trimmed. As we worked on the design, we began to see that rather than representing mere aesthetic differences, these conflicts symbolized the complexity of the Penns' relationship and personalities. We realized that the two contrasting themes and the tension between them could become a vital source of the architecture — the task was to express the contrasts boldly while uniting them into some sort of whole.

The lot was long and narrow, gently sloping down toward a wonderful view of the San Francisco Bay to the west. The lot dictated a long, thin house placed along the east/west axis. Our first design decision was to locate the building as close as possible to the street — much closer than the adjacent houses — to minimize narrow side yards and provide the house with spacious views into neighboring yards rather than into neighboring windows. We contrasted the front and back yards by almost cutting the site in two with the widest part of the house (but still keeping the linking space in good proportion). At the same time, we defined the entry court with a wall of the building. We then twisted the house slightly on the site to open up the entry court to the street for clarity and to preserve an old acacia tree as the centerpiece of the court.

The entry and its relationship to the rest of the house is perhaps the most dramatic expression of the building's contrasting themes of in/out, exposed/tempered and residential/industrial. Designed as a two-story glass house, the light, airy structure splits the solid house in two. Downstairs, it separates the common spaces in the west from the utility spaces (workshop, garage, guest bathroom) in the east; upstairs it runs between the parents' and the children's spaces. The

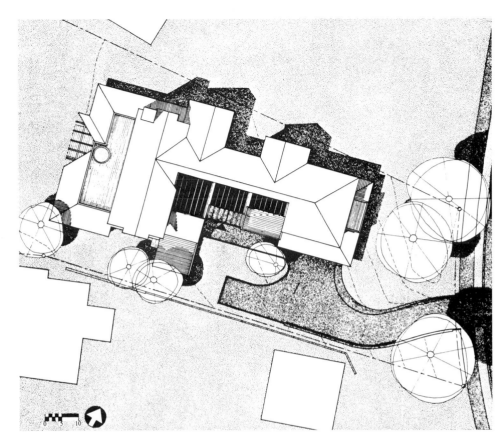

The house is located closer to the street than the neighboring houses to allow more views to the side. An old acacia tree was preserved in the entry court to contrast with the new house.

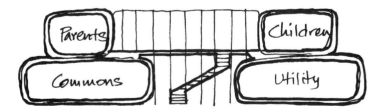

The central two-story glass entry connects the divided house. A handcrafted wood staircase winds up through this industrial-like space to a second-level bridge.

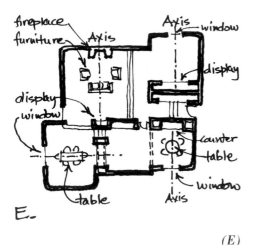

fireplace
furniture
Axis
Axis — window
display
display
window
counter table
table
Axis — window
Axis

E.

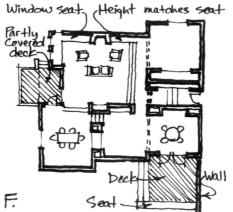

Window seat
Height matches seat
Partly Covered deck
Deck
Wall
Seat

F.

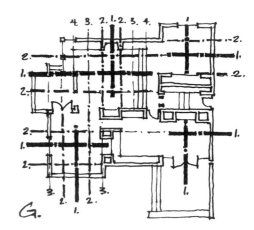

4. 3. 2. 1. 2. 3. 4.

G.

(E)
Give each subsidiary area an axis to help center it and make it feel more solid and substantial.
(F)
Link the inside to the outside with decks and a window seat.
(G)
Link each of the spaces by aligning the primary axis of symmetry of one space with the secondary or tertiary axis of symmetry of its neighbor.

To increase the sense of solidity of each of the smaller spaces, we centered them with subsidiary axes of symmetry, established with such elements as a fireplace, display niche, major window or major piece of furniture (E). This symmetry also enhances the feeling of formality, elegance and order of each area.

Linking the interior spaces to the exterior was accomplished by creating exterior decks, by extending existing walls out into the landscape and by projecting window seats (F). We gave the decks compact, squarish shapes just like the rooms and further defined them with walls and roofs so they would be partly inside, partly outside. Note how the window seat in the living room matches the height of the music room, completing the symmetry around the fireplace.

We completed the plan by connecting each space with lower levels of symmetry, by aligning the second-level or third-level axis of symmetry in one space with the first-level or second-level axis of symmetry in another (G). These aligning axes are then expressed architecturally with ceiling beams above. Take the living-room/dining-room relationship, for example. The living room has a primary north/south axis (through the middle of the fireplace), followed by secondary and tertiary axes of symmetry. The same is true for the dining room, and what is interesting here is that the tertiary north/south axis of the living room corresponds to (or lines up with) the primary north/south axis of the dining room. Similarly, the primary east/west axis of the music room corresponds to the secondary east/west axis of the living room, linking those two spaces. In general, these interconnecting axes link all of the various spaces, and this interconnection contrasts with the centeredness of each space.

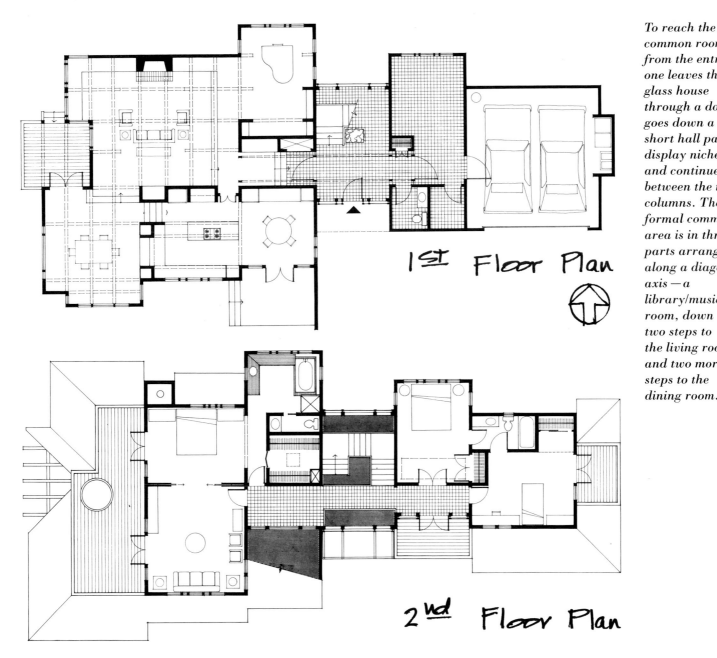

1ˢᵗ Floor Plan

2ⁿᵈ Floor Plan

To reach the common rooms from the entry, one leaves the glass house through a door, goes down a short hall past a display niche, and continues between the two columns. The formal commons area is in three parts arranged along a diagonal axis — a library/music room, down two steps to the living room and two more steps to the dining room.

Another aspect of the plan worth noting is that the three main parts of the living/entertainment area (music room, living room and dining room) lie along a diagonal axis, with all three spaces visible, and therefore linked, to one another. The vertical axis is also involved: The living room is two steps down from the music room, and the din-

The dining room is the lowest room in the house, and the most formal. It is centered by the high ceiling beams and the single arched window, echoed on the opposite wall by an arched opening to the kitchen. (Photos by Mark Jacobson.)

ing room is two steps down from the living room. The dining room is the lowest spot along the axis and, with its high ceiling, the most formal. Its formality is punctuated with the one arched window in the house. This window in turn sets up an arched opening to the kitchen, bringing in light, which is matched in the breakfast room with a great splash of light from the glass-house roof above.

Upstairs, east of the bridge, are the bedrooms and balconies for the children. The first bedroom, on the north, steals light from the glass house through an interior skylight. The other bedroom has a private balcony cut into the roof below. Since the east end of the house is dug in 4 ft., the roof and balcony feel suprisingly close to the ground — you can easily jump down. West of the bridge is the couple's realm. It consists of a large sun room for sitting and working; a space for a bed, which can be joined to the sun room with large sliding doors; a large bathing room; and finally, a long deck to the west, which connects these spaces and provides spectacular views of the San Francisco Bay.

Once the design of the house had been determined, we continued to search for ways to link the primary contrast between a solid, established, residential house and a transparent, contemporary, industrial house. The corrugated cement-asbestos panels selected for the roof incorporate both images simultaneously. This material is generally used in industrial applications, but its corrugated texture is similar to the texture of clay tiles, a material that is typically associated with residential construction.

The roofing caps a rather muted color scheme. From the street, the grey-brown stucco walls rise from a paving of black-brown bricks to the white-grey Transite roof with its charcoal-colored gutters and downspouts. Part of the rationale for such a tightly controlled color spectrum is that the neighborhood contains many similarly colored houses. But color schemes need some contrasting sparkle, and in the Penn house this is provided by the warm, reddish-tan color of cedar trim and by a cool band of deep blue tile which wraps around the house. The blue color begins as a cap detail on the extended wall at the entrance courtyard, proceeds into the entry as a stair-rail detail, winds up the stairway and then wraps around the building like a ribbon at the sill height of the second story, continuing around the balconies as a railing detail.

The idea for the contrasting blue stripe came while we were building an early model. We wanted to indicate a possible change of material at the second-story sill line, and because we were in a rush, we tacked some blue carbon paper to the cardboard to represent the idea. When Carol Penn saw it, she said, "What's this blue stripe?" We apologized for the inept model. "No," she said, "It's great—let's do it in blue tile." So we did.

The overall cool, muted colors of the paving, walls and roof are punctuated by the warm color of wood trim and the cool blue tile band, which starts at the entry court, continues up the stair rail, emerges as a deck rail and wraps the building at mid-height.

The industrial-style aluminum windows are linked to the residential interior with mullions of wallboard and wooden sills. (Photo by Mark Jacobson.)

The industrial laminated beams were integrated with the residential interior by exposing the natural warm color of the Douglas fir laminations and by trimming the ends with decorative cuts. (Photo by Mark Jacobson.)

The window details were also designed to unite the contrasting images of the house. First we mixed materials and details, using exposed rough-cedar framing and fine wood stairway detailing within the industrial glass house (see the photos on p. 66 and p. 116), and bronze-anodized aluminum windows in the solid house. We then tempered these contrasts and sewed them into the fabric of adjacent building materials. For example, the aluminum windows in the solid house were set into a framework of large-scale mullions formed out of the wall itself and trimmed at the sill with smooth cedar, all to integrate and link the harsh metal with the soft residential interior.

The exposed ceiling beams throughout the common spaces were another attempt to unite residential and industrial themes. Sometimes the beams are structural, sometimes they're purely decorative. (One of the secondary beams between the music room and the living room actually hangs from higher beams, making visible its purely decorative role.) To express this contrast, we used laminated beams, which are normally exposed only in industrial or commercial construction. We gave them a transparent finish to make visible their industrial source, but then had decorative arcs cut at their ends for a Craftsman touch.

The Winslow House

Lafayette, California
Architect: Barbara Winslow

This project was a large (2,500-sq. ft.) addition to the country home of Barbara Winslow. Here, Winslow describes her design process.

This house began when my husband and I heard about eight acres of land for sale in an isolated canyon in the hills of San Francisco's East Bay. Tired of suburban tract-house living, we had been looking for a house with more connection to nature and less to a neighborhood. The lot was just what we sought: A canyon site with a small creek at the bottom, it included a large, flat site for gardens and a yard, and stables on a rolling hillside. Steep, oak-covered hills on each side of the canyon created a sense of real isolation. The only sounds were those made by crickets, frogs and chickens; at night we could see no lights but our own. But the existing house on the lot was far less delightful — a mint-green, four-room, concrete-block rectangle. It was relatively solid and contained indoor plumbing, but offered little else. We bought the property immediately.

Trained in the theory that you can best design for a site by living on it, my five-person family moved into the four rooms of the "old house." The idea was to begin almost immediately on plans for a new house, but it was obvious that the old house would have to be made more livable if we were to survive in it until a new home was complete. We embarked on two years of upgrading — opening ceilings, adding attic loft beds for the kids, replacing plumbing fixtures and appliances, painting and adding storage. When I was finally ready to focus on plans for the new house, my vision of the project was extremely nearsighted. I was living in the midst of a system plagued with problems of space and trying to design from that perspective.

Sitting at the office working on plans, I could envision a new whole. I wanted to treat the old house as an appendage, perhaps turn it into a guest house, and create a new building with none of the problems of the old. The first plan I devised was a grand house sitting higher on the hill. But none of us could imagine living in it; moving away from the old house felt like abandoning a family member. The second scheme concealed the old house as a bedroom wing behind the new structure, but the balance between the buildings still felt wrong. Living on the site had made us conscious of the potential of the existing house, and we were unwilling to settle for a plan that didn't fit its surroundings.

The new and old parts of the home work together to create a courtyard with a strong form of its own.

To the gardens

Old house   New house

The materials of the house are simple and rustic: brown shingles, red corrugated-steel roof, wood doors and windows. The house sits comfortably in its country setting. (Photo by David Petersen.)

Time was growing tight. The building season was about to begin, so the final design was created in two weeks with a sense of "now or never." When I worked intuitively, the new house became a contrasting partner with the old—mates across a courtyard—and the rooms fell into place around this scheme.

The choice to divide a home into two parts around a court is an unusual one. In this case, it was undoubtedly a reaction to two years of excessive closeness, with far too little privacy. Yet it made perfect practical sense. The children were becoming adolescents, with musical tastes beyond comprehension and a need for a place they could call their own. A teenage cottage, close to the authority, safety and nurturance of the parent house, was a good choice for our family at this stage of life. Later, the separate wing could become a rental unit. Once the basic organization was defined, it became important to link the two elements strongly and express their underlying continuity.

The separation of the buildings establishes several dichotomies, the first of which is the contrast between the old and the new. The teenage cottage is the old house, built 40 years earlier. The main house is new, still being finished. The link between them, the trellis, is made of hand-shaped new wood, which sits

124

on four old redwood columns salvaged from the porch of an early 1900s bungalow. The intermingling of old and new in the courtyard symbolically links the buildings and establishes a theme pursued throughout the main house. Salvaged building parts create special places: an arched French door/window decorates the living room, old Tuscan columns define the inglenook, stained-glass panels beautify the space above the kitchen sink and a schoolhouse window lights the desk in the master bedroom.

The second major dichotomy is the contrast between in and out. The original house was experienced as a strong "in" in a field of "out." The block walls have small openings and give a feeling of solidity, which provides complete separation from the outdoors. The new complex of buildings has a completely different feel. The courtyard that links the "in" portion of both buildings is a true indoor/outdoor space. Roofed by the trellis, which relates to the exposed ceiling joists of the interior, and floored with red brick, which relates to the interior tile, this courtyard is still fully exposed to the elements. Because it acts as a passage, it constantly brings people outdoors. We choose to be inside knowing just what it is like outside. And we are linked by the view from in to out to in again as we look across the court.

The old Tuscan columns on each side of the inglenook announce it as a special place in the midst of this new construction. (Photo by David Peterson.)

The French doors of the dining room look across the courtyard to matching doors in the family room of the teenage cottage; on nice days, the whole space can be opened into an enormous indoor/outdoor room. (Photo by David Peterson.)

125

South elevation

The balcony off the master bedroom offers a view into the gardens or down into the courtyard below.

The first-floor plan reveals the organizing geometry of the new house. Every room is systematically planned and lies on a major or minor axis. The plan of the second floor is open but includes a small alcove where one can retreat into a private space.

Also distinguishing the two buildings are the contrasts between high and low, and big and small. While the teenage cottage is small and low (a slab floor right at grade; 8-ft. ceilings; single-story; broad, flat plan; separated, enclosed rooms), the new house is bigger and taller. It is perched just above a steep 25-ft. drop to a creek, and views to the north are into tall treetops. Its organization is vertical. Ceilings are high, open to the slope of the roof, and are accentuated by clerestory windows. The second story of the new house is open to the space below through an open stair hall. The original house offered no high spaces, no place to get above it all, an absence amply compensated for by the new house. The plan incorporates a balcony that overlooks the courtyard, visually joining the high and low buildings so that both can be experienced simultaneously.

A major characteristic of the years before we built was a perennial sense of disorder. We lived in the midst of the inevitable chaos of a busy family life, working parents, ongoing projects and numerous pets. When there is not enough time or enough space to put everything away, I need to sense an overall order in the structure of the house that is greater than the clutter of daily living. Plans for the new house began therefore with a strong sense of spatial order established by a consistent use of geometric axes and sub-symmetries, compensation for the order missing in daily life. Almost every space in the building is symmetrical within itself, and most of these small symmetries fall on the axis of a larger symmetry.

Thus you approach the house through a central courtyard, which is roughly symmetrical and which ends in a symmetrical brick patio defined by columns at the four corners that hold up the open trellis. This formal outdoor space is flanked on each side by entries—one to the new adult house, one to the old teenage cottage.

The new house is cruciform in organization. The long axis (A in the drawing on the facing page) runs from the kitchen to the living room, and is anchored at each end by special windows—a large arched window in the living room and an assembly of six windows, topped by stained glass, in the kitchen. A short axis (B) is devoted to dining, stair circulation and a wood-burning stove. Here also the ends of the axis are marked by special windows—French doors in the dining area and a window seat at the stairway landing. Where the two axes meet (the heart of the house) there is a sitting area at the foot of the stairs, which is heated by the woodstove and surrounded by cooking and eating spaces.

The order of the plan can also be felt in the structure, which is organized by a post-and-beam system set up on an alternating pattern of 8-ft. and 12-ft. spans. All the rooms are related in scale by these dimen-

The long axis through the house ends in a tall arched window looking over the creek. (Photo by David Peterson.)

127

In the spring, wisteria blossoms cover the trellis and the brick floor of the patio, softening the lines of the structure. (Photo by David Peterson.)

house and courtyard. Internally, we still feel the disorder of the earlier years and constantly see reminders of it in the old house.

The links between order and mystery are numerous, but subtle. The yard between the houses is designed as a garden in the English cottage style, gaining a sense of order from its borders, patterns of colors and pathways, yet allowing each plant its natural form and growth. This garden is linked to the surrounding wild landscape by the incorporation of native plants. The trellis with its strong spatial order of beams and crosspieces is a small-scale example of this dynamic. In spring, the wisteria vine grows rampantly over the trellis, covering it with blossoms, yet the form is directed and confined by the structure; the real pleasure of the space comes from this mix of man and nature.

The final contrast to be found is in the area of open/closed. All rooms in the old house were fully closed, defined spaces, separated by doors and controlled by locks. The new house is open along its entire length. Rooms flow into one another through half-walls or freestanding columns. Spaces are implied rather than outlined. The only interior doors are on closets and bathrooms. Yet each room is strongly defined. A living room is formed by two adjoining rectangles, which are

sions, and in space by the wooden beams and posts, which form a visible structural skeleton throughout the house. On a smaller scale, floor/ceiling joists are exposed along the building's spine in a repetitive pattern, and the floors throughout are gridded by tiles in traffic areas.

The overall sense is clearly one of order. Where then is the contrast? The disorder? In this case, it is everywhere else: The house is situated in a wild, overgrown canyon with an organic order of its own. A sense of natural chaos surrounds the defined at the open end by posts and a half-wall. This area, for sitting, music and dance, is sensed as an independent whole, because it has its own roof form, its shapes are geometrical and its floor is formed by a large square of softwood—the dance floor—bordered by a pattern of ceramic tile, which also paves the inglenook. The dining area is also marked by posts and half-walls at its outer edges, while the space gains form from a symmetrical arrangement of windows, a lamp creating a pool of light over the table, a simple square plan and an ornamental tile pattern expressing the center line.

Even the entry, a simple space, gains an identity from the half-walls and columns, which stand to each side of the doors, and from the special ornamental tiles arranged diagonally at the center of the space.

The open spaces also allow an easy retreat into the more confined spaces. From the living room it is possible to be comfortably enclosed in the inglenook—the roof is lower, the space is filled with built-in seats, the front edge is defined by a beam and a half-wall, and windows are small. In contrast to the openness of the living space, the inglenook is cavelike. Similarly, the master bedroom includes a low-ceilinged alcove for retreat and meditation; inside this small area

you are out of sight of the large main space, private and alone, yet still connected.

The linkage of open and closed spaces, their meeting at walls half-open, half-closed, provides a real choice—it is possible to be in the midst of the action or to retreat and be solitary yet see what is happening—without the limitations of conventional rooms. It was this desire for a balance between traditionally extreme contrasts that both consciously and intuitively informed all aspects of this design, from site plan to choice of materials.

The fire burning in the inglenook's fireplace can be seen from the whole living area, an invitation to enter this small, cavelike space. (Photo by David Peterson.)

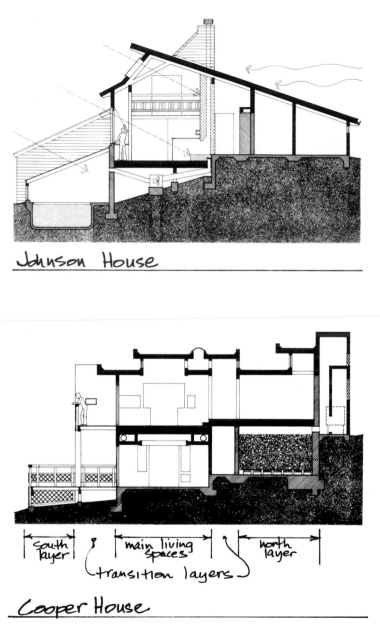

As energy-efficient designs, the Johnson (top) and Cooper (bottom) houses share several characteristics, but they have entirely different looks. The foggy climate of the Johnson site allows less aggressive overhangs on the south than are required for the harsher sun of the Cooper site.

Johnson House

south layer | transition layers | main living spaces | north layer

Cooper House

The Johnson House
The Cooper House

Northern California; San Ramon, California
Architects: Jacobson, Silverstein

A house is primarily a response to the personality, needs and aspirations of the client, but its design is also powerfully shaped by the climate and site. The available sunlight, prevailing breezes and outdoor temperature range affect the building's position on the site and the arrangement of its roof, walls and windows. We designed these houses for two very different clients, but the projects shared an important similarity—both clients wanted their houses to conserve energy, using sunlight for heating, outside air for cooling and thermal mass for temperature stabilization.

In general, energy-efficient houses must mediate between climatic extremes, storing energy from the sun for use during cooler periods. They derive their efficiency from capitalizing on the differences between northern and southern exposures, day and night, winter and summer, solid and void. The Johnson and Cooper houses share fundamental organizational strategies. Each sits on an open south-facing slope in a rural setting. Each has a low story on the north side, which contains the main entry and service spaces (laundry, guest bedroom) and few windows (to conserve energy loss during cold weather). These low north facades look rather empty and mysterious, like the back of a building. By contrast, on the south the houses open up to two or two-and-a-half stories. These sides, which are covered with large expanses of glass, contain the main living spaces. As well as being tall, they are light, full and ordered. But the two houses are worlds apart in the images they project. They also use different types of thermal storage. The Johnson house uses massive concrete-block walls to store the day's heat passively, while the Cooper house employs an active system of circulating air through a "room" full of rocks.

Architects often worry that the buildings they design when working under tight constraints will not have the individuality they seek. The Johnson and Cooper houses offer evidence that solar houses don't have to comply with an established image. The primary contrasts here —north/south, tempered/exposed, order/mystery and light/dark — are strongly determined by solar orientation and energy-conscious strategies. But while these things do constrain designers, they do not limit the result, and each house expresses itself needs in a dramatically different way.

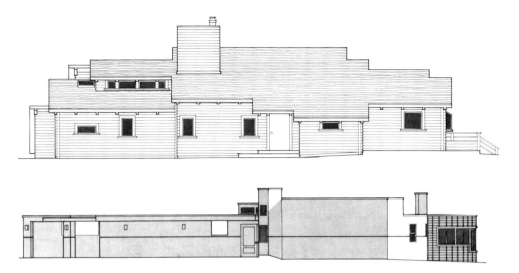

In both homes, entrances are located on the blank north facade, which creates a feeling of mystery; the visitor knows little about the house until the door is opened.

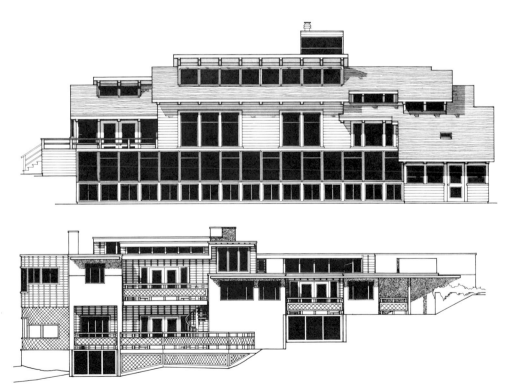

The south facades of both houses share qualities of openness, complexity, fullness of detail and the sense of order that is generated by the various divisions of windows and doors.

The Cooper house was conceived as a brown wood house wrapped and protected by a white stucco shell. On the south side, cedar wood trellises and decks project out beyond the stucco toward the sunshine, extending the living space and shading it from the summer sun.

The Cooper House

The climate at this site, located many miles from the coast, is usually moderate: Winters are short with many sunny days, and hot summer temperatures are modulated by cool evening breezes. It is an excellent site for a passive-solar building.

The hill upon which the house sits slopes to the southwest, yet optimum solar gain demands a due-south orientation. These two contrasting axes, 37° apart, were overlaid and became the framework for the development of the plan. Toward the north, the driveway, garage, entry, rock room (literally a room full of rocks that act as a thermal reservoir) and bedrooms nestle along and in the contour of the slope. These spaces are housed in a simple, closed, mysterious form expressed in dense, solid white stucco. The opposite side of the building is shaped by the sun, full of sun-catching decks and balconies. The form, strongly ordered by the modular elements of standardized windows and 16-in. o.c. framing, is complex and open to the sun. Linking the two axes together is a third geometry, the semicircular arcs generated by the rotation of the axis from south (sun) to southwest (slope). These arcs can be seen in the east and west walls of the secondary bedrooms and baths, and again in the main south deck. To contrast with the linear geometry of the building, we extended the use of the arcs to describe smaller, semicircular forms, which surround the west-facing kitchen porch, the hot tub and the master sleeping area.

Because the climate here is both hotter and colder than on the coast, the contrasts are more extreme. One way we responded to this was to create different layers of space, each tempering the microclimate of its neighbors (refer to the floor plans on the facing page and the section on p. 130). For example, the building is dug into the ground on the north side, which helps cool the comparatively dark and cavelike rooms in that part of the house during the summer (this also tempers them from the extremely cold winter temperatures). These rooms are lit from clerestory windows; this light, entering from above, intensifies the cavelike feeling of the rooms. Within this northernmost layer is the active cooling system — the rock bed — which is precooled each summer evening by cool night air. During the hot day, interior air can be circulated through the rock bed and cooled by the thermal mass of the rocks. The contrasts of the climate — too hot, too cold — are linked and tamed by this thermal storage.

The southernmost layer consists of wood exterior decks, patios and trellises. Fully exposed to the sun to capitalize on good weather, this layer serves as a shade to the rest of the building. The main living spaces are sandwiched between these two layers and buffered by transition zones. The first zone, linking the south decks with the main living spaces, consists of tiny interior spaces (stair landing, study alcove, the master bedroom's tub room) and of semi-enclosed secondary decks. Each of these spaces, interior or exterior, has a south-facing overhang, either solid or filtered. The second buffering transition zone, which links the north layer with the main spaces, consists of circulation space, defined by free-standing posts and stairs down into the living area.

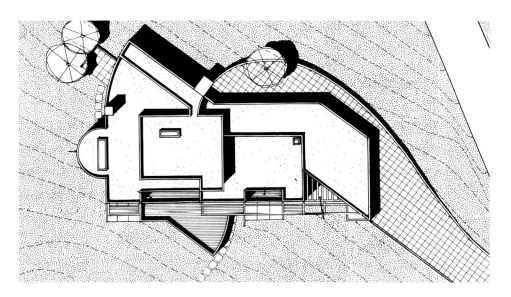

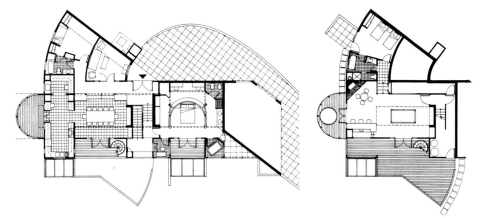

Two contrasting geometries are at work in the house. The main living spaces of the house are set due north/south, while the foundation and base of the house are dug into the slope, which lies at 37° west of south. It is a split-level design with the garage, entry, guest bedrooms and bath, kitchen and living/dining room all on the upper level; the master bedroom and bath are one-half level down, and the family room and extra bedroom are a full level below.

The semicircular form on the west side of the house contains an interior sitting room upstairs and an exterior hot-tub space downstairs. The curved wood siding gradually opens up to link the inside/outside contrast.

Group Housing Projects

In addition to custom-designed single-family houses, we have also worked on several group-housing projects over the years. It is beyond the scope of this book to discuss them in detail, but it is interesting to indicate some of the ways contrast theory is useful in the design of multi-unit residential projects.

Santa Rosa Creek Cooperative

Santa Rosa, California
Arthitects: Jacobson, Silverstein

This complex, containing 25 low-income housing units, was designed for a group of seniors who were working to develop simpler and more communal ways of life than multiple-family housing normally permits. As a result of this goal, perhaps the most powerful issue that shaped the project was the contrast between the public realm and the private world.

To create this contrast, we divided the site into three parts. The first, just off the street, contains the parking area. Visitors and residents leave cars and traffic behind as they proceed from this area to the second one — an open commons space containing a meeting room, a mail port and the community gar-

One final note: In the semicircular form on the west of the building, we linked the enclosed kitchen porch upstairs with the outdoor hot tub below by manipulating the exterior wall siding. Upstairs it consists of tightly joined horizontal boards, which form a solid wall. But as they continue down toward the hot tub, each board is narrowed, creating increasingly wide spaces between, until there is more space than siding, and the resulting hot-tub space is essentially outdoors.

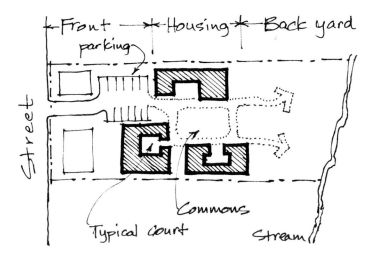

Front ← Housing → Back yard
parking

Street

Commons

Typical court

Stream

The long, skinny lot of the Santa Rosa Creek Cooperative is divided into three sections: the front public parking area, the rear private backyard and the housing itself, which links front and rear together. The housing is also organized into three parts: the common space in the middle, the three housing units that surround it and the building courts, which link each building to the center.

At the Santa Rosa Creek Cooperative, the view from the courts looks out onto the larger common areas.

dens, surrounded by three buildings containing the private housing. The third and rearmost area is a large, undisturbed backyard, its farthest edge defined by Santa Rosa Creek. Thus, the central housing and commons form a link between the street life on one side and the natural world on the other.

To link the secondary contrast between the central commons and the private housing, we gave each building an outdoor entry court, which opens to the larger central commons beyond. These courts act as a sub-commons for each of the buildings, containing the stairs and bridgeways to the units, as well as some upper decks. They are informal meeting places for the people who live in each of the buildings.

The long housing blocks of Hilltop Terraces tightly enfront an urban street, containing all vehicular traffic, parking and entrances to the units. Each unit also has access to a rear greensward through cascading balconies that lead down to the ground via stairs.

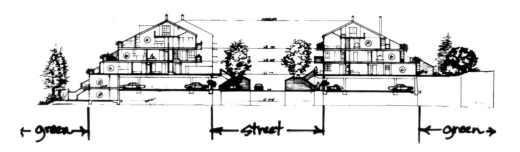

← green →   ← street →   ← green →

Section through the Housing Units

This view of the street shows how the units directly enfront one another; the mix of car and pedestrian traffic helps to create a dense, lively city street.

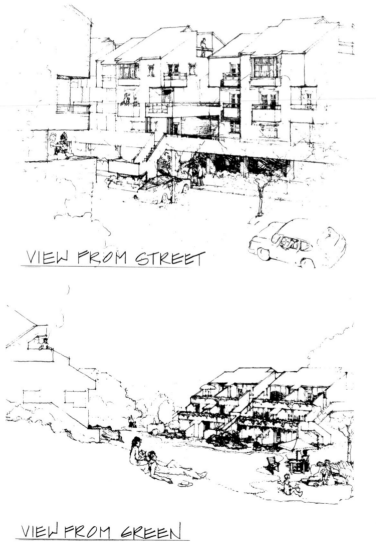

VIEW FROM STREET

Each unit's rear outdoor space cascades down into the flowing open green space that winds through the development.

VIEW FROM GREEN

Hilltop Terraces (proposed in 1985)

Richmond, California
Architects: Jacobson, Silverstein, Winslow

The drawings on this page illustrate an unbuilt schematic design for 1,000 residential rental units on a 15-acre parcel, created for a developer interested in purchasing the property. Even in this schematic stage, the project provides an interesting study in the contrast between city and country, street and park, front and back.

Because the housing density is high (67 units per acre), we first attempted to tame the automobile. Our approach was to concentrate it in certain areas, enabling other areas to be quieter and more natural. Foregoing the usual attempts to soften the streetscape with large areas of landscaping, we opted instead for a more urban environ-

138

ment, where all of the parking garages and entrances to the units are located directly on the access street. To enable people and cars to coexist on this narrow street, we connected all the housing blocks with an elevated pedestrian walkway.

This concentration of traffic on the front side of the buildings allowed the creation of a park-like greensward at the back. These sloping open spaces wind continuously through the site and are accessible from all the units.

The blocks of housing link these two areas. Each unit has a front entrance on the street, but also backs onto the green with a private balcony over the unit below, linked directly to the green by stairs or a private yard on grade.

Student Housing, World College West

Petaluma, California
Architects: Jacobson, Silverstein, Winslow

Student dorms, almost by definition, have to be rather spartan. In spite of a limited budget, we felt that the small individual rooms had to be contrasted with the drama and excitement of a larger community space.

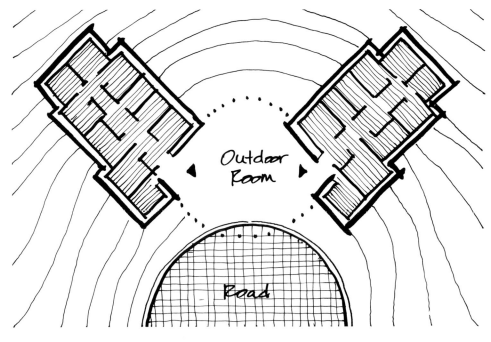

The site is at the end of a cul-de-sac, overlooking a beautiful view of the rolling hills beyond. To preserve the view that a building would normally block and to contrast the natural landscape more strongly with the man-made road and building, we broke the dorm in two and bent the halves away from each other at a 45° angle. The opening between the buildings becomes a framed view; the 45° angle draws onlookers forward into the space between the buildings to get yet a better view. But even more important, splitting the building apart creates a large, strongly shaped void in between, a space that becomes both an outdoor room and a grand entrance to the buildings.

The dorm building at World College West was broken in half and opened up at a 45° angle to create a grand, open entry and public outdoor room. The solid buildings, containing enclosed, small private rooms, are best used to shape a larger, open public space.

139

The void between the buildings at World College West is linked to the buildings by 'furnishing' the space with entrances, stairs, balconies and a bridge. To complete the sense of this space as an outdoor room, a fireplace was added to the design along the axis of symmetry.

Though the structure is still incomplete, one can feel the sense of a public room created between the buildings.

To link the void to the buildings, we projected the circulation among the buildings into this space; that is, we populated it with human action and presence. We placed the main entrances to each building on this forecourt, as well as the exterior stairs, and added a bridge to connect the buildings. As a final touch to all these furnishings, we located an outdoor fireplace and inglenook along the axis of symmetry, thereby inviting students to pause in their comings and goings and gather together before retiring to the privacy of their rooms.

Construction of the dorms had to proceed in stages as money became available from donors. The buildings are now complete, save for the connecting bridge and outdoor fireplace. Still, enough has been built that the outdoor room exists as a real presence.

Madera del Presidio Subdivision

Corte Madera, California
Architects: Jacobson, Silverstein,
Winslow

This design is for a 160-unit development of single-family homes, duplexes and triplexes. The site has both sloping and flat lots, with good views to the San Francisco Bay and the surrounding ridgelines. Because the site is so visible from the surrounding town, there is concern in the community that the development make a positive contribution to the overall townscape.

From our point of view, we face a dual problem. On the one hand, how do we economically create the variety, richness and contrast that are often missing from subdivisions? On the other hand, how do we gracefully link all the various units to create unity and lend order to the whole?

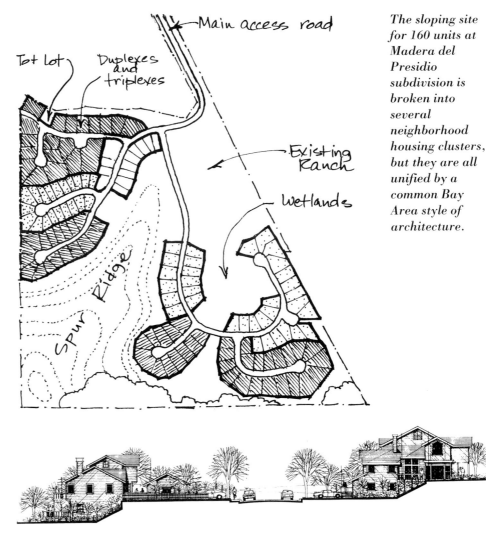

The sloping site for 160 units at Madera del Presidio subdivision is broken into several neighborhood housing clusters, but they are all unified by a common Bay Area style of architecture.

This sketch of a typical street in the Madera del Presidio subdivision illustrates the eventual character of the development after five to ten years of landscape establishment.

141

These different designs, shown on pp. 142-144, all share a common stylistic linkage, although there is tremendous variation in layout.

We aren't sure that we will succeed at our goal of achieving linked contrast in a project of this scale. At this writing, the work is still in the preliminary stages. Indeed, we are right in the middle of the fray, with city planners, design-review boards, our client and a dozen consultants all pushing and pulling on the project.

We began our work by remembering that the criticism of "sameness" is generally not leveled at neighborhoods in a traditional pre-industrial town, even though the house type, basic design and materials used are repeated from unit to unit. No design-review board would ask the builders of a Greek village to alter the facades from unit to unit simply to create variety. Indeed, such indigenous townscapes seem to possess an almost perfect balance of contrast and variety, with an overall linking unity.

So the issue here seems to be not the avoidance of sameness, but finding an appropriate sameness —what kind of unifying sameness could create a foil for the expression of contrasting differences in this project?

In this development, we are using the "Bay Area Style" as the unifying and linking theme. Some of its elements are:

informal, asymmetrical floor plans and facades;

compact, two-story volumes with secondary protuberances and attachments;

gently sloping roofs with exposed framing at the overhangs;

modestly sized casement windows;

exterior walls of wood and stucco sheathed with wood, accented at the base with stone or stucco.

Against this overall linkage of style, contrast is generated by offering 13 models and a palette of door, trim and roof colors — on pp. 142-144 are examples of several of the models. In spite of their different floor plans, they have been designed as part of one stylistic family. The drawings also show that additional variety and contrast can be obtained by using different wood skins — vertical board and batten, horizontal siding or shingles — or by using different materials, such as stone or stucco, at the base of the buildings.

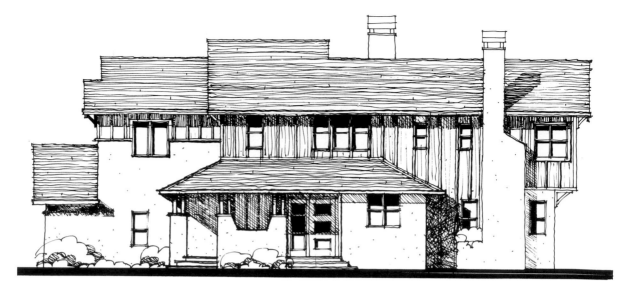

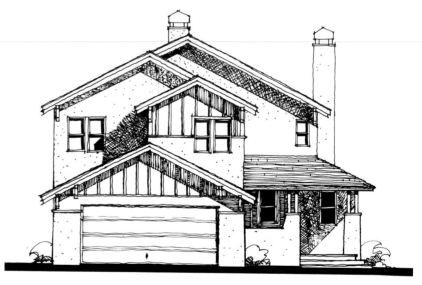

We also looked to the role of color for an additional important source of contrast. Our starting point was the color of the composition roof shingles, which consists of a mixture of gravels — each shingle has some black, dark grey, light grey, warm red-brown, warm tan-brown and cool blue-green particles. (The percentage of each of these colors determines the perceived color of the shingles.) All subsequent color decisions would ultimately come back to these shingles.

We selected a transparent stain for the cedar siding that is lighter than the dark roof shingles, and linked the siding to the roof by choosing a tint that is already present to some degree in the shingles. For the window, door and rafter trim, we chose a slightly tinted grey as a transition between the dark roof, lighter siding and lightest window and sliding-door frames. The tint of the grey was derived from the roof particles. The color for the brick paving leading to the front porch was selected to repeat the darkness and hue of the roof, leaving the lighter wall color sandwiched in between the two.

These broad areas of color are all earthy tones, which means that the colors are not very saturated. But each building needs a small, sharply contrasting spot of real color to spark up the whole composition (a little like using a dash of hot sauce to give a dish some zing). We chose the front door as the appropriate location for some deeply saturated color. For each palette, we offered two choices — a warm hue and a cool hue — but even here we derived the color from the color of the roof shingles.

Each of the color palettes is linked to the contrasting colors of the gravel particles in the roof shingles and to the white of the window frames.

Song of Salt and Pepper

Dinner twins,
who remind us that nothing
we know of remains uncoupled or
unparalleled, you revolve from hand to hand,
place to place, like seasons circling
each other in different hemispheres,
converging and married on our evening plates.
One of you, the center of the sea and tears,
reminds us that there is no food
we eat without a bitterness,
that pleasure stings and is
endured like pain;
your mate burns our food, and blisters
our mouths, buries in our meat
its devouring flavor, a carnivore
like us, feeding in darkness and in heat.
May the two of you remain in nightly wedding,
teaching us an equal taste for dark and light,
salt spraying white upon our meal like day,
pepper grinding black its accompanying night.

— Patricia Storace

from *The New Yorker*
March 9, 1987

Permissions

Frontispiece: From *Native American Architecture*, by Peter Nabokov and Robert Easton. ©1988 by Peter Nabokov and Robert Easton. Reprinted by permission of Oxford University Press, Inc.

Photo, page 5: Collection of WESTPAC, photo by Kate Flynn.

Photo, page 8: From *The Japanese House*, by Tatsuo Ishimoto. ©1963 by Crown Publishers, Inc. Reprinted by permission of Crown Publishers, Inc.

Photo, page 22: From *Patios & Gardens of Mexico*, courtesy of Architectural Book Publishing Co., Inc.

Plan, page 25: from the W. W. Wurster Collection, courtesy Richard Peters.

Photos, page 25, 31, 95 and 98: © The Oakland Museum, Oakland, Calif.

Photos, pages 28, 90 and 93: Courtesy Documents Collection, College of Environmental Design, University of California, Berkeley.

Photo, page 44: Alinari/Art Resource: 23821.

Photo, page 62: From *By Shaker Hands*, by June Sprigg. ©1975 by June Sprigg. Reprinted by permission of Alfred A. Knopf, Inc.

Drawings, pages 94, 96 and 97; and photos, pages 99 and 100: Courtesy Architectural Drawings Collection, University of Texas at Austin, permission of Harwell Hamilton Harris.

Poem, page 146: Reprinted by permission; © 1987 Patricia Storace. Originally in *The New Yorker.*

Editor: Laura Tringali
Designer: Deborah Fillion
Layout artist: Cathy Cassidy
Copy editor: Peter Chapman
Production editor: Ruth Dobsevage
Art assistant: Iliana Koehler
Computer-applications specialist: Margot Knorr
Print production manager: Tom Greco

Typeface: Bodoni
Paper: Warrenflo, 70 lb., neutral pH
Printer and binder: Ringier America, New Berlin, Wisconsin